Greed Is Good

Greed Is Great

Greed Is Good

Maximization and Elite Deviance in America

Matthew Robinson and Daniel Murphy

ROWMAN & LITTLEFIELD PUBLISHERS, INC.
Lanham • Boulder • New York • Toronto • Plymouth, UK

ROWMAN & LITTLEFIELD PUBLISHERS, INC.

Published in the United States of America
by Rowman & Littlefield Publishers, Inc.
A wholly owned subsidary of The Rowman & Littlefield Publishing Group, Inc.
4501 Forbes Boulevard, Suite 200, Lanham, Maryland 20706
www.rowmanlittlefield.com

Estover Road
Plymouth PL6 7PY
United Kingdom

Copyright © 2009 by Rowman & Littlefield Publishers, Inc.

British Library Cataloguing in Publication Information Available

Library of Congress Cataloging-in-Publication Data

Robinson, Matthew, 1970–
  Greed is good : maximization and elite deviance in America / Matthew Robinson and
Daniel Murphy.
    p. cm.
  ISBN-13: 978-0-7425-6070-3 (cloth : alk. paper)
  ISBN-10: 0-7425-6070-8 (cloth : alk. paper)
  ISBN-13: 978-0-7425-6071-0 (pbk. : alk. paper)
  ISBN-10: 0-7425-6071-6 (pbk. : alk. paper)
  eISBN-13: 978-0-7425-6578-4
  eISBN-10: 0-7425-6578-5
  1. White collar crimes—United States. 2. Avarice. 3. Anomy. I. Murphy, Daniel, 1970–
II. Title.
  HV6769.R63 2009
  364.16'80973—dc22   2008025218

Printed in the United States of America

♾ ™ The paper used in this publication meets the minimum requirements of American
National Standard for Information Sciences—Permanence of Paper for Printed Library
Materials, ANSI/NISO Z39.48-1992.

To my Mom and Brother, Randa and Brandt Robinson, who helped me learn to look up instead of down. Thanks!

—Matthew Robinson

To my Mom and Dad, Richard and Janet Murphy, who not only gave me life, but saved my life. Remember the fun (!) factor!

—Daniel Murphy

Contents

Preface

The saying "greed is good" was popularized in the 1987 film *Wall Street*. The film was made during a time when greed in the corporate world was rampant, and when greed in America was promoted and even widely celebrated. Amazingly, in spite of the well-known corporate crimes committed during that era, including the savings and loans (S&L) scandals, the sad fact is that greed appears more popular and corporate crime more widespread than ever in the United States.

In this book, we offer a theory of corporate criminality called contextual anomie/strain theory. The theory asserts that corporate crimes are motivated by greed, which arises out of dual pressures exerted on individuals by institutions in American society, as well as within the corporation itself. The theory is a new, general theory of crime, which integrates anomie and strain theories with elements of conflict, learning, social control, personality, and opportunity theories.

The goal of the book is to introduce our theory of corporate criminality and to show how it can explain the most serious crimes facing our nation—elite deviance. The book is divided into six chapters. In chapter 1, we identify key realities of crime that any theory of crime should be able to explain: that crime is normal, that most crime is property crime, and that corporate crime is far more dangerous than street crime. We also introduce the concepts of greed and "maximization" and show how these are the key concepts of our theory.

Maximization lies at the heart of our theory and refers to the concomitant utilization of legitimate and illegitimate means of opportunity in pursuit of wealth. That is, maximization occurs when elites use illegal means simultaneously with legal means to achieve their goals of wealth or profit. The concept of maximization is the inductive prodigy of research that explored perceived stringency in punishment compared to actual punishment as delineated in the United States Sentencing Commission Guideline Manual. Our original research presented respondents with a set of vignettes and queried what the appropriate punishment should be for each criminal act described. Punishments suggested by respondents were compared to the actual punishment prescribed in the Guideline Manual.[1]

In our earlier research, we noted an anomaly in prescribed sentencing, as compared to Guideline dictates, for a vignette in which a contractor built a bridge, illegally breaking code in pursuit of profit, while simultaneously operating a legitimate business. The outcome of the illegal behavior perpetrated by the contractor was the collapse of the bridge and the deaths of five motorists. Consistently respondents indicated "the contractor should have a fine imposed," "the contractor should have his license revoked," "perhaps it was the workers' fault and not that of the contractor," and so forth. We were struck by the lengths the respondents went to justify the illegal activities of the contractor: acts that led to the deaths of five human beings. We realized that the contractor was working toward the socially inculcated goal of the American Dream (legitimate means of opportunity), thus justifying the illegal actions of cutting corners in construction and breaking code (illegitimate means of opportunity). This led to the development of the "maximizer," one who concomitantly incorporates legitimate and illegitimate means of opportunity in the pursuit of profit and/or monetary gain (the American Dream).[2]

In chapter 2, we summarize the major anomie and strain theories. Then we show how our theory fills a key gap left by the works of scholars like Robert Merton, Steven Messner and Richard Rosenfeld, and Richard Cloward and Lloyd Ohlin. Two main differences separate our theory from theirs. First, as noted previously, our theory posits that people abide by the law (conformity) and break it (innovation) simultaneously, and this adaptation to strain is normal in certain contexts in society (e.g., corporations). No anomie or strain theorist had explicitly recognized this adaptation to strain. Second, our theory is explicitly aimed at elite deviance, which is far more damaging than the street crimes traditionally explained by anomie and strain theories.

In chapter 3, we introduce our theory of crime—contextual anomie/strain theory. We lay out its main propositions and show how greed is central to the theory. We also summarize the literature on corporate culture in order to illustrate how and why criminality is so common within the nation's businesses.

In chapter 4, we apply the theory of contextual anomie/strain theory to corporate crimes such as fraud and false advertising. Then in chapter 5, we apply the theory of contextual anomie/strain theory to corporate activities such as defective products and manufacturing tobacco. In these two chapters we introduce various forms of corporate crime, describing them in detail with specific examples. We illustrate how they involve maximization and then demonstrate how our theory explains these behaviors.

In chapter 6, we summarize the theory and identify crime prevention implications of the theory. We also discuss how the issues we raised in the book relate to *social justice*, a topic that has been typically ignored by other criminological theorists.

NOTES

1. Murphy, Daniel, and Matthew Robinson (2008). The maximizer: Clarifying Merton's theories of anomie and strain. *Theoretical Criminology* 12(4): 501–21.

2. Murphy and Robinson, The maximizer.

1

Introduction to Greed, Maximization, and Crime

Greed is good.

—Actor Michael Douglas, playing Gordon Gekko,
largest stockholder at the fictional paper company Teldar Paper,
in a speech to stockholders from the film *Wall Street* (1987).[1]

The opening quote is part of a long speech given by the lead movie character Gordon Gekko: "Greed . . . is good. Greed is right. Greed works. Greed clarifies, cuts through, and captures the essence of the evolutionary spirit. Greed, in all of its forms; greed for life, for money, for love, knowledge, has marked the upward surge of mankind. And greed, you mark my words, will not only save Teldar Paper, but that other malfunctioning corporation called the USA."

The 1980s are commonly referred to as the "me decade" and even by some as the "greed decade." For example, authors Stephen Rosoff, Henry Pontell, and Robert Tillman write that "the 1980s have been viewed retrospectively as the decade when greed came out of the closet. The love of money, which once 'dared not speak its name,' refused to shut up."[2] David Simon agrees, claiming that the 1980s and 1990s were "a period in which the individual focus was on self-concern, personal survival, and greed. This personal focus was aided and abetted by a conservative, probusiness administration that somehow made greed seem moral and corruption an everyday fact of political life."[3]

This was a time when U.S. Presidents Ronald Reagan and George H. W. Bush staunchly defended "supply-side economics" and deregulation of industry to allow the "free market" to grow the U.S. economy through "personal

1

freedom." Reagan and Bush believed that the collective striving for personal wealth by millions of Americans was good for the U.S. economy. So, it makes sense that the film *Wall Street* was produced in 1987.

Only two years after the release of this film, Michael Milken was convicted of numerous counts of securities violations for illegal activity related to utilizing high-yield bonds (aka "junk bonds") to encourage corporate mergers and acquisitions and to generate massive profits.[4] After being indicted on ninety-eight counts, Milken ultimately pleaded guilty to only six crimes, including unlawful security transactions, tax fraud, and insider trading, among others.[5]

It is easy to see the case of Michael Milken as an example of greed, for Milken was already in possession of everything any person needs (and then some) when he engaged in his illegal activities in pursuit of even greater wealth. Greed is defined as "a selfish and excessive desire for more of something (as money) than is needed,"[6] or "excessive or rapacious desire, esp. for wealth or possessions."[7] Yes, Michael Milken was greedy.

When a person is referred to as greedy, it is usually meant as an insult, because greed is typically viewed in a negative light (as in "selfish" or without regard for the needs of others). Greed is typically seen as a vice and is even listed as one of the seven deadly sins of Catholicism. In spite of this, greed somehow has also become accepted and even celebrated as a good thing in American society.

Milken's case is evidence of this; in spite of profiting in the hundreds of millions of dollars through his illegal activity, Michael Milken's prison sentence was a mere ten years. This was later reduced to only two years by the same judge who originally sentenced him, in part because Milken assisted with other investigations. Additionally, although the *New York Times* noted in an editorial that Milken's sentence was appropriate and sent a strong signal that corporate deviance would now finally be taken seriously in the United States, another editorial by the *New York Times* justified some of what Milken did in an effort to help many Americans achieve greater wealth.[8] As if this was not enough, after being released from prison, Milken later began teaching a business course at the University of California, Los Angeles (UCLA)![9]

Today, Milken is a multibillionaire and one of the five hundred richest people in the world. Later charges by the Securities and Exchange Commission (SEC) alleged that Milken participated in the securities industry after being banned from it in 1991. Milken received tens of millions of dollars for providing advice to major corporations in the 1990s. Although he ultimately paid the money back, Milken did not receive any further punishment. And so, greed is still good in America today. It is still justifiable in the context of the American Dream.

MAXIMIZATION AND THE AMERICAN DREAM

In this book, similar to other anomie theorists, we argue that the American Dream promotes criminality.[10] The American Dream refers to "a broad cultural ethos that entails a commitment to the goal of material success, to be pursued by everyone in society, under conditions of open, individual competition."[11] In essence, the American Dream means achieving wealth; in fact, according to anomie theorists, the American Dream means achieving more wealth than you already have, regardless of how much you have. Viewed in this light, greed is part of the American Dream because it calls for achieving far more than one needs. In this book, we will explain how greed is related to the American Dream and how this can promote criminality.

While other prominent anomie theorists such as Robert Merton, Steven Messner, and Richard Rosenfeld have already posited that the American Dream is criminogenic, we offer a new mechanism through which this operates—maximization. *Maximization* refers to the concomitant utilization of legitimate (i.e., legal) and illegitimate (i.e., illegal) means to achieve the goals associated with the American Dream. Thus, maximization occurs when individuals utilize strategies of "conformity" and "innovation" simultaneously.[12] Stated differently, maximization means abiding by the law and violating it at the same time. Much of what we call maximization can also be described as greed. An example is a board of directors of a corporation (which by definition is involved in legal activity) deciding to ignore workplace safety regulations (an illegal activity) in order to "maximize" profits. When this occurs, especially when workers get sick, injured, or killed, this type of maximization can be described as greedy.

As we show in chapter 2, anomie theories explain criminality as a function of a precedence being placed on *goals* associated with the American Dream (e.g., wealth) over the *means* to achieve those goals (e.g., work). Thus, typically, anomie theorists see criminals as those who have abandoned legitimate means such as work in favor of more "innovative" means such as crime. While there is evidence that this does occur, this explanation is typically limited to various forms of street crime (e.g., dealing drugs).[13] Further, proponents of this approach do not explicitly consider the possibility that there are situations in American society that permit and sometimes even require individuals to break the law while simultaneously engaging in legal activity such as work. Thus, we lay out our argument that the American Dream promotes criminality by providing justification for illegal activity in the context of legal activities like employment.

In this book, we offer a new, general theory of crime, one centered on the concept of maximization. As we argue later, we strongly believe our theory has wide scope, in that it explains not only most forms of criminality in the United States, but also its most harmful forms. We now turn to the issue of crime and the particular forms it takes in America. Here, we lay out the reality of crime in the United States and state basic facts of crime that any theory should be able to explain.

THE NATURE OF AMERICAN CRIME

Although images of crime are widespread in the media, the perceptions of crime held by Americans are inaccurate in at least three significant ways. First, people tend to assume that criminals are different from noncriminals (when in fact everyone is a criminal). Second, when people think of crime, they tend to think of violent crime (even though the vast majority of crime is property crime). Third, people are most afraid of street crime (even though the most dangerous crime is committed by elites).

With regard to the first point, even from the earliest self-report studies conducted—where potential offenders are asked about their involvement in criminality—studies have shown that virtually everyone is a criminal.[14] Criminologist Tom O'Connor notes: "The results of most self-report studies are shocking. They typically indicate, that for any population (even a law-abiding one), about 90 percent of the people in the sample have committed a crime for which the punishment is more than a year in prison."[15]

Amazingly, even professional criminologists admit to committing various forms of crimes. A study of criminologists affiliated with the American Society of Criminology (ASC) examined forty-four forms of crimes, deviance, and ethical violations. The study focused on "serious" crimes of the Uniform Crime Reports (UCR), drug-related crimes, acts of sexual deviance, fraud-related crimes, computer crimes, occupational crimes and deviance, and other ethical violations.[16]

Findings showed that criminologists are criminals too. For example, 66 percent of criminologists admitted to having driven drunk at some point in their lives, 60 percent to illicit drug use, 55 percent to theft, 36 percent to verbal assault, 25 percent to physical battery, 23 percent to adultery, 22 percent to burglary, 19 percent to tax fraud, 3 percent to rape, and 2 percent to robbery. While the numbers declined with regard to current criminality (committed in the past twelve months), the point is that even highly educated professionals who study crime for a living—a large portion of whom have earned doctoral degrees—admit to committing a wide array of criminal, harmful, deviant, and unethical behaviors.

Matthew Robinson and Barbara Zaitzow, authors of the study, note that "these . . . data demonstrate that we criminologists are to a degree, what we study—i.e., we commit acts of crime and deviance. Depending on the type of behavior being referred to, many criminologists admit both to having committed them in the distant past and in the past twelve months, including many which are codified as 'serious' and 'harmful' in the criminal law. . . . Crime and deviance [are] normal, even among criminologists."[17]

Some people start committing crimes earlier than others (i.e., in early childhood), most start later (i.e., in adolescence). Some commit more serious crimes than others, most commit less serious crimes. Some persist in crime over their entire lives, most mature out of crime.[18] So, there are differences in the nature and extent of offenses committed by criminals; yet, it is clear that we are all criminals. This suggests, as long ago posited by Émile Durkheim, that crime is normal. In the words of Durkheim: "Crime is present not only in the majority of societies of one particular species but in all societies of all types. There is no society that is not confronted with the problem of criminality. Its form changes; the acts thus characterized are not the same everywhere; but, everywhere and always, there have been men who have behaved in such a way as to draw upon themselves penal repression."[19]

Not only is street crime normal in the United States, we've long known that corporate crime is normal. For example, Edwin Sutherland's classic study of seventy of the largest corporations in the United States found that every one of them had violated the law at least once, with the average number of known violations being fourteen. Further, 98 percent of the corporations were recidivists, or repeat offenders, and 60 percent had been convicted of criminal offenses in courts.[20] Amazingly, corporate crime is even more widespread today than back in Sutherland's day.[21]

If criminality is normal, criminological theory must take this fact into account. Any theory that posits causes of crime to be "abnormal" (e.g., head injury, parental abuse, etc.) should be considered as meant to explain "abnormal" behaviors (e.g., impulsive assault, murder) and thus incapable of explaining most crimes—the vast majority of which can be considered "normal" in the context of modern American society.

With regard to the second point about the nature of crime, research demonstrates that when Americans think of crime, they tend to think of violent crime. In fact, the great bulk of crime in any given year is committed against property, and the most common form of property crime in the United States is simple theft. For example, the Federal Bureau of Investigation (FBI) reports that in 2005 there were 6,776,807 thefts known to the police, which represented 58.6 percent of all crimes known to the police in that year. Property crimes (theft, burglary, and motor vehicle theft) made up 88 percent of all crimes known to the police in 2005. If one added in robbery, a violent crime aimed at gaining property, the percentage of crimes committed against property rose to 91.6 percent of all crimes.[22]

These crime data are from the Uniform Crime Reports (UCR), a source that includes only crimes known to the police. Yet, data from the National Crime Victimization Survey (NCVS) depict a similar picture. For example, 2005 NCVS data show that 77 percent of all criminal victimizations were committed against property.[23] When robbery and purse snatchings are included, property crimes made up 80.6 percent of all victimizations in 2005.[24] When one adds property loss due to corporations' illegal and deviant behaviors, more than 99 percent of all crime is likely property crime. Later in this chapter, we show just how much corporate crime costs Americans.

If criminality is primarily committed against property, criminological theory must take this into account. Any theory that can only explain violent crime cannot explain sources of property crime and thus is incapable of helping us understand most crime.

Regarding the third point, Americans are under the impression that the greatest threat to their personality safety and property comes from below—the poor. This is a myth.[25] In reality, the greatest threats to the health and welfare of American citizens come from above—the wealthy.[26] This is another way of saying that *street crimes* (those crimes disproportionately committed by the poor and middle class) are actually not as dangerous as *corporate and white-collar crimes* (those crimes committed disproportionately by the wealthy).

Table 1.1 depicts the estimated amount of money lost to street crimes versus corporate and white-collar crimes. As you can see, acts of elite deviance are far more damaging than street crime. *Elite deviance* is a term put forth by David Simon in his book of the same name.[27] It includes not only criminal acts but also unethical acts, civil and regulatory violations, and other harmful acts committed intentionally, recklessly, negligently, or knowingly. Elite deviance is a term that encompasses *white-collar crime,*[28] *corporate crime,*[29] *corporate violence,*[30] *occupational crime,*[31] *governmental deviance,*[32] *crimes of the state,*[33] *crimes of privilege,*[34] *profit without honor,*[35] and those *crimes*

Table 1.1.   Property Damages Caused by Street Crime versus Corporate and White-Collar Crime

Street Crime	$20 billion
White-Collar and Corporate Crime	$404 billion

Source: Reiman, Jeffrey (2006). *The Rich Get Richer and the Poor Get Prison* (8th ed.). Boston, MA: Allyn & Bacon.

by any other name[36] committed by our *trusted criminals.*[37] These are acts that cause tremendous physical, financial, and moral harms to Americans.

Since there is no national data source on white-collar and corporate crime, the figure from table 1.1 represents an estimate from one of the top scholars studying forms of *elite deviance* in the United States.[38] With regard to the $404 billion figure, we are confident of two things. First, it is a conservative estimate of the true costs of white-collar and corporate crime. Second, there is no question that whatever the true amount, white-collar and corporate crime is far more damaging than street crime.

Our book concerns itself with perhaps the worst crime of all—corporate crime. Wade Rowland, author of *Greed, Inc.*, asserts: "We all know that corporations frequently behave in deeply antisocial ways. Drug companies conceal unfavorable test results. Oil companies despoil the environment. Clothing companies exploit child laborers. Automobile companies knowingly market vehicles with deadly design flaws. Media companies pump out violence for children." Further, when corporations get busted for their transgressions, the first response is typically to "lie their way out—they lie, in fact, habitually, in advertising for their products and services and in their public relations communications."[39]

Other examples of corporate wrongdoing include "the corporate lobby against measures to reduce the impact of global warming; corporate practices that are environmentally destructive; corporate dislocation of people's lives through 'rationalization' measures; corporate exploitation of Third World workers; corporate participation in the worldwide illegal arms traffic; corporate concealment of harmful side effects of widely used pharmaceuticals; systematic corporate tax evasion (impoverishing the public sector); corporate suborning of information media; corporate promotion of the excesses of consumerism," and so on.[40] All of this is far more damaging than street crime.

Amazingly, the U.S. government is aware that some forms of elite deviance are more damaging than some forms of street crime. For example, losses caused by personal theft are far less than $20 billion per year. Yet, as shown in table 1.2, the Department of Justice, Office for Victims of Crime, reports significant losses due to the crime of fraud.

Fraud is a form of theft whereby a person is deprived of his or her money or property through deceit, trickery, or lies. This means fraud involves two moral wrongs—theft and deceit. Yet, police in the United States are most focused on property crimes committed on the streets (e.g., theft) while far less resources are devoted to fraud.[41] This is surprising given the relative damages caused by each form of theft. It's also surprising given the high likelihood that fraud occurs far more frequently than theft.

Table 1.2. Losses Due to Fraud

The Internet Fraud Complaint Center reported a $54 million loss in 2002, making a significant change from the $17 million loss in 2001. Of the people who filed claims to the IFCC, only 1 in 4 had contacted law enforcement. (National White Collar Crime Center. 2003. *2002 Internet Fraud Report.* Richmond, VA)

Securities regulators estimate that securities and commodities fraud totals approximately $40 billion a year. (National White Collar Crime Center. 2003. *Securities Fraud.* Richmond, VA)

Check fraud is estimated to cost U.S. businesses $10 billion a year. Experts anticipate a 2.5 percent increase in check fraud losses each year. (National White Collar Crime Center. 2002. *Check Fraud.* Richmond, VA)

Consumers and others lose an estimated $1 million hourly—$40 billion annually—to telemarketing fraud. In 2002, the average loss due to telemarketing fraud was $845. (National White Collar Crime Center. 2003. *Telemarketing Fraud.* Richmond, VA)

Insurance fraud costs the U.S. economy $80 billion each year, according to the Coalition Against Insurance Fraud. (National White Collar Crime Center. 2002. *Insurance Fraud.* Richmond, VA)

Source: U.S. Department of Justice. Office for Victims of Crime. Costs of crime and victimization. Retrieved July 30, 2007, from www.ojp.usdoj.gov/ovc/ncvrw/2004/pg5b.html.

While theft requires face-to-face contact with a criminal (or direct contact with a person's property), fraud can be committed any time there is a property transaction. That is, any time someone buys, sells, or trades something, there is a potential for fraud. Fraud can also occur when a person takes any product in for service (e.g., automotive repair fraud) or when a service person is called to repair a product (e.g., VCR/DVD repair fraud). Because of this, many criminologists are convinced that fraud is the most common crime in the United States.

Fraud is widespread. A recent survey by the FBI of 2,066 organizations found that 64 percent suffered some financial loss from computer fraud in the past year. The average loss per company was more than $24,000. After extrapolating such losses to only 20 percent of all business in the United States, a very conservative estimate of computer fraud from the FBI suggests it costs about $67 billion per year.[42] Based on a study by Javelin Strategy & Research, the same report suggests that identity fraud costs about $52.6 billion per year.[43]

Even if you are not very good at math, it is pretty easy to see that such forms of elite deviance clearly outweigh all direct losses caused by street crime. In order to protect oneself from fraud, a person would have to know everything about every product and service he or she buys, sells, trades, or owns, for only this would preclude the chance of being ripped off during a property transaction. This is impossible, which is one reason why fraud is so widespread.

Table 1.3.   Deaths Caused by Street Crime versus Corporate and White-Collar Crime

Deaths from Street Crime (2005)	
Murder	16,692[a]

Deaths from White-Collar and Corporate Crime	
Tobacco use	438,000[b]
Obesity	112,000[c]
Hospital error	100,000[d]
Occupational disease and injury	55,000[e]
Unsafe and defective merchandise	30,000[f]

Sources:
[a]Federal Bureau of Investigation http://www.fbi.gov/ucr/05cius/.
[b]Department of Health and Human Services. Centers for Disease Control and Prevention. Fact Sheet. Cigarette smoking-related mortality. Retrieved July 30, 2007, from www.cdc.gov/tobacco/data_statistics/Factsheets/cig_smoking_mort.htm.
[c]Department of Health and Human Services. Centers for Disease Control and Prevention. CDC's national leadership role in addressing obesity. Retrieved July 30, 2007, from www.cdc.gov/doc.do/id/0900f3ec803207fd.
[d]Institute of Medicine (2000). *To Err Is Human*. The National Academies Press. www.nap.edu/books/0309068371/html.
[e]Reiman, Jeffrey (2006). *The Rich Get Richer and the Poor Get Prison* (8th ed.). Boston, MA: Allyn & Bacon; Robinson, Matthew (2009). *Justice Blind? Ideals and Realities of American Criminal Justice* (3rd ed.). Upper Saddle River, NJ: Prentice Hall.
[f]Robinson, Matthew B. (2006). Defective products. *Encyclopedia of Corporate and White-Collar Crime*. Golson Books and Sage Publications.

Elite deviance not only costs more in terms of financial loss than street crime, it is also far more deadly. Table 1.3 shows the estimated number of deaths caused by various forms of behaviors (some illegal and some not). As you can see, acts of elite deviance are far more damaging than street crime.

Corporate violence is different in some key ways from violence on the streets of America. Table 1.4 illustrates these differences. First, whereas violent street crime is direct, corporate violence is indirect. That is, the latter does not involve one person directly hurting another but instead "results from policies and actions, undertaken on behalf of the corporation, that result

Table 1.4.   Corporate Violence versus Street Violence

Street Violence	*Corporate Violence*
Direct	Indirect
Immediate harm	Delayed harm
Individual offender	Multiple offenders
Various motivations	Financial motivation
Intentional	Culpable

in the exposure of people to harmful conditions, products, or substances."[44] Second, whereas violent street crime results in an immediate harm, harms from corporate violence occur days, weeks, months, and even years after the corporate decisions are made.

Third, whereas violent street crime is typically committed by one person acting alone or in conjunction with a small group of closely knit people, corporate violence involves "a large number of individuals acting collectively."[45] For example, murder involves the "killing of *one human being by another*." Other forms of killing like those listed in table 1.3 are typically perpetrated by numerous individuals (e.g., boards of directors of corporations) or large numbers of other individuals. Fourth, whereas street violence can be motivated by financial gain, corporate violence is "virtually by definition . . . motivated by the desire to maximize corporate profit (or survival) and minimize corporate overhead."[46]

Finally, whereas street violence typically results from *intentional* acts, corporate violence results from other kinds of culpable behaviors and "is a consequence rather than a specifically intended outcome."[47] For example, tobacco companies obviously do not intend to kill any particular person, nor do fast food companies that make, market, and sell foods high in calories and saturated fat. Similarly, doctors and hospital staff, employers, and manufacturers of defective products typically do not kill people on purpose. That is, people do not die from cigarettes, conditions related to obesity, hospital error, occupational disease and injury, or unsafe products because of the *intentional* acts of corporations. Yet, deaths produced by these acts are still the result of culpable acts.

Culpable means "meriting condemnation or blame especially as wrong or harmful."[48] Culpable acts include those behaviors that are committed negligently, recklessly, and knowingly. *Negligence* refers to behaviors that are committed as a result of a failure to meet normal or recognized expectations. An example is failing to follow safety regulations meant to protect human life, which results in death. *Recklessness* refers to behaviors that are committed without due caution for human life or property. An example is forcing employees to work in dangerous conditions. Acts committed *knowingly* refer to behaviors committed with knowledge that an outcome is likely. An example is continuing to manufacture a product after product testing reveals a high likelihood of a deadly defect.[49]

The primary difference between murder and the other forms of killing in table 1.3 is that murder is intentional. The FBI defines murder as "the *willful* (nonnegligent) killing of one human being by another."[50] When an act is done willfully or intentionally, it is committed with "a guilty mind" (*mens rea*) and on purpose. An example of a murder is when a man kills his wife with a gun after an argument or for insurance money.

Many of the deaths in table 1.3 result from the negligent, reckless, and knowing behaviors of elites—corporate executives, food companies, doctors, employers, and manufacturers; therefore, they are good examples of culpable killings. Although it is true that acts committed with intent are generally considered more serious than those committed negligently, recklessly, or knowingly, people killed by big tobacco, food companies, as well as reckless and negligent doctors, employers, and product manufacturers are just as dead as those murdered. This is why many view those killed by such behaviors victims of serious crimes as well.[51]

Further, American citizens are strongly influenced by the actions of elites—including corporations—through their advertising campaigns for products such as cigarettes, fast food, and other products. Although victims of elite deviance sometimes play a role in their own victimizations (e.g., smokers choose to smoke, people choose to eat too much fast food), they do so under heavy influence from the efforts of the corporations who make a killing (literally) by selling their products. Interestingly, criminologists have shown that many victims of street crime also play a role in their own victimization.[52] Yet, when a man kills his girlfriend after years of abuse even though the victim chose to remain in the relationship, society does not excuse the killer's behavior. Similarly, when a person is murdered after leaving the windows in his home unlocked, the police still pursue the murderer. Thus, you might question the logic of ignoring the killer in cases of elite deviance just because he or she is a corporate executive and commits his or her killings indirectly and from afar.

As it turns out, criminal law is inherently biased against the poor.[53] This is because the criminal law is written by the wealthy, lobbied for (and against) by the wealthy, and disproportionately voted for by the wealthy. This means that "the label of 'crime' is applied to only a small portion of acts that are harmful to Americans." Further, the "label of 'serious' crime is reserved for those acts that the government perceives to be committed primarily by the poor."[54] The result? Far greater focus in the United States on street crime rather than on elite deviance, even though the latter is far more dangerous.

It is not just criminal justice that is disproportionately focused on street crime; criminological theories are also generally aimed at explaining street crime. This is problematic precisely because street crime is not nearly as dangerous as elite deviance. Thus, criminological theories cannot explain the worst crimes in America and are thus seriously limited in their scope. If criminal victimization means "any act that produces financial or physical harm and is committed intentionally, negligently, recklessly, or knowingly," then forms of elite deviance identified here should be considered crimes.[55] And if they are considered crimes, criminological theory ought to be able to explain such acts.

In this book, we offer a theory of crime that takes into account three key facts: (1) crime is normal, (2) most crime is committed against property, and (3) elite deviance is far more dangerous than street crime. Further, our theory is aimed at explaining a key form of elite deviance—corporate crime—and thus has the potential to explain the largest share of criminality in the United States.

In the next chapter, we discuss our concept of maximization, explain how we developed it, how it is related to anomie theories and the American Dream, and how greed plays a key role in its justification. We also lay foundation for application of the concept of maximization to that type of crime we view as the most dangerous of all—corporate crime. Later in this book, we examine property crimes committed by corporations (chapter 4) as well as violent acts committed by corporations (chapter 5).

NOTES

1. IMDb (2007). Memorable quotes for *Wall Street*. Retrieved July 27, 2007, from www.imdb.com/title/tt0094291/quotes.

2. Rosoff, Stephen, Henry Pontell, and Robert Tillman (2002). *Profit Without Honor: White-Collar Crime and the Looting of America* (2nd ed.). Upper Saddle River, NJ: Prentice Hall, 454.

3. Simon, David (2006). *Elite Deviance* (8th ed.). Boston, MA: Allyn & Bacon, 30.

4. Stewart, James (1991). *Den of Thieves*. New York: Simon & Schuster.

5. Bruck, Connie (1988). *The Predators' Ball: The Inside Story of Drexel Burnham and the Rise of the Junk Bond Raiders*. New York: Simon & Schuster, 1988.

6. Merriam-Webster Online Dictionary. Entry for "greed." Retrieved July 25, 2007, from www.merriam-webster.com/dictionary/greed.

7. Dictionary.com. Entry for "greed." Retrieved July 27, 2007, from dictionary.reference.com/browse/greed.

8. Messner, Steven, and Richard Rosenfeld (2001). *Crime and the American Dream* (3rd ed.). Belmont, CA: Wadsworth, 1–2.

9. Messner and Rosenfeld, *Crime and the American Dream*.

10. Merton, Robert (1957). *Social Theory and Social Structure*. Glencoe, IL: The Free Press; Messner and Rosenfeld, *Crime and the American Dream*.

11. Messner and Rosenfeld, *Crime and the American Dream*, 5.

12. Murphy, Daniel, and Matthew Robinson (2008). The maximizer: Clarifying Merton's theories of anomie and strain. *Theoretical Criminology*, 12(4): 501–21.

13. Robinson, Matthew (2004). *Why Crime? An Integrated Systems Theory of Antisocial Behavior.* Upper Saddle River, NJ: Prentice Hall.

14. For an excellent summary of classic and contemporary self-report studies, see Terence Thornberry and Marvin Krohn (2003). Comparison of self-report and official data for measuring crime (43–94). In John V. Pepper and Carol V. Petrie (eds.), *Measurement Problems in Criminal Justice Research.* Washington, DC: National Academies Press.

15. O'Connor, Tom (2005). Crime data. Retrieved August 1, 2007, from faculty.ncwc.edu/toconnor/111/111lect02.htm.

16. Zaitzow, Barbara, and Matthew Robinson (2001). Criminologists as criminals. In Alex Thio and Thomas Calhoun (eds.), *Readings in Deviant Behavior.* Boston, MA: Allyn & Bacon.

17. Robinson, Matthew, and Barbara Zaitzow (1999). Criminologists: Are we what we study? A national self-report study of crime experts. *The Criminologist* 24(2):17.

18. Farrington, David (2005). *Integrated Developmental and Life-Course Theories of Offending.* Newark, NJ: Transaction; John Laub and Robert Sampson (2006). *Shared Beginnings, Divergent Lives: Delinquent Boys to Age 70.* Boston, MA: Harvard University Press; Terrie Moffitt (1993). Adolescent-limited and life-course-persistent antisocial behavior: A developmental taxonomy. *Psychological Review* 100: 674–701; Terrie Moffitt (1997). Adolescent-limited and life-course-persistent offending: A complementary pair of developmental theories (11-54). In T. Thornberry (ed.), *Developmental Theories of Crime and Delinquency, Advances in Criminological Theory.* Newark, NJ: Transaction; Robert Sampson and John Laub (2005). *Crime in the Making: Pathways and Turning Points through Life.* Boston, MA: Harvard University Press.

19. Durkheim, Émile (1895, 1982). *Rules of the Sociological Method.* New York: Free Press, 65.

20. Sutherland, Edwin (1973). Crime of corporations. In Schuessler, Karl (ed.), *On Analyzing Crime.* Chicago: University of Chicago Press.

21. Clinard, Marshall, and Peter Yeager (1980). *Corporate Crime.* New York: The Free Press.

22. Federal Bureau of Investigation. Uniform Crime Reports (2005). Table 1: Crime in the United States by volume and rate per 100,000 inhabitants, 1986–2005. Retrieved July 30, 2007, from www.fbi.gov/ucr/05cius/data/table_01.html.

23. U.S. Department of Justice, Office of Justice Programs, Bureau of Justice Statistics. Criminal victimization. Retrieved July 30, 2007, from www.ojp.usdoj.gov/bjs/cvictgen.htm.

24. U.S. Department of Justice, Office of Justice Programs, Bureau of Justice Statistics. Criminal victimization in the United States, 2005, statistical tables. Table 1: Number, percent distribution, and rate of victimizations, by type of crime. Retrieved July 30, 2007, from www.ojp.usdoj.gov/bjs/pub/pdf/cvus05.pdf.

25. Kappeler, Victor, and Gary Potter (2004). *The Mythology of Crime and Criminal Justice* (4th ed.). Long Grove, IL: Waveland Press.

26. Reiman, Jeffrey (2006). *The Rich Get Richer and the Poor Get Prison* (8th ed.). Boston, MA: Allyn & Bacon; Matthew Robinson (2009). *Justice Blind? Ideals and Realities of American Criminal Justice* (3rd ed.). Upper Saddle River, NJ: Prentice Hall.

27. Simon, David (2005). *Elite Deviance* (8th ed.). Boston, MA: Allyn & Bacon.

28. Sutherland, Edwin (1977a, 1977b). White-collar criminality. In Gilbert Geis and Robert Meier (eds.), *White-Collar Crime: Offenses in Business, Politics, and the Professions*. New York: The Free Press.

29. Clinard, Marshall, and Peter Yeager (2005). *Corporate Crime*. Edison, NJ: Transaction.

30. Frank, Nancy, and Michael Lynch (1992). *Corporate Crime, Corporate Violence*. Albany, NY: Harrow and Heston.

31. Blount, Ernest (2002). *Occupational Crime: Deterrence, Investigation, and Reporting in Compliance with Federal Guidelines*. New York: CRC.

32. Erman, David, and Richard Lundman (2001). *Corporate and Governmental Deviance: Problems of Organizational Behavior in Contemporary Society* (6th ed.). New York: Oxford University Press.

33. Michalowski, Raymond, and Ronald Kramer (2006). *State-Corporate Crime: Wrongdoing at the Intersection of Business and Government*. Camden, NJ: Rutgers.

34. Shover, Neil, and John Wright (2000). *Crimes of Privilege: Readings in White-Collar Crime*. New York: Oxford University Press.

35. Rosoff, Stephen, Henry Pontell, and Robert Tillman (2006). *Profit Without Honor: White-Collar Crime and the Looting of America* (4th ed.). Upper Saddle River, NJ: Prentice Hall.

36. Reiman, *The Rich Get Richer*.

37. Friedrichs, David (2006). *Trusted Criminals: White Collar Crime in Contemporary Society* (3rd ed.). Belmont, CA: Wadsworth.

38. Reiman, *The Rich Get Richer*.

39. Rowland, Wade (2005). *Greed, Inc.: Why Corporations Rule Our World and How We Let It Happen*. Toronto, Canada: Thomas Allen Publishers, xix–xx.

40. Rowland, *Greed Inc.*, 109.

41. Robinson, Matthew (2005). *Justice Blind? Ideals and Realities of American Criminal Justice* (2nd ed.). Upper Saddle River, NJ: Prentice Hall.

42. News.com. Computer crime costs $67 billion, FBI says. Retrieved July 30, 2007, from news.com.com/Computer+crime+costs+67+billion,+FBI+says/2100-7349_3-6028946.html.

43. Javelin Strategy & Research. www.javelinstrategy.com.

44. Friedrichs, David (1995). *Trusted Criminals: White Collar Crime in Contemporary Society*. Belmont, CA: Wadsworth, 70.

45. Friedrichs (1995), *Trusted Criminals*, 70.

46. Friedrichs (1995), *Trusted Criminals*, 71.

47. Friedrichs (1995). *Trusted Criminals*, 71.

48. Merriam-Webster Online Dictionary. Entry for "culpable." Retrieved July 31, 2007, from www.merriam-webster.com/dictionary/culpable.

49. Robinson (2005). *Justice Blind?*

50. Federal Bureau of Investigation. Murder. Retrieved August 1, 2007, from www.fbi.gov/ucr/05cius/offenses/violent_crime/murder_homicide.html.

51. Karmen, Andrew (2006). *Crime Victims: An Introduction to Victimology* (6th ed.). Belmont, CA: Wadsworth.

52. Felson, Marcus (2002). *Crime and Everyday Life* (3rd ed.). Beverly Hills, CA: Sage.

53. Shelden, Randall (2007). *Controlling the Dangerous Classes: A History of Criminal Justice in America* (2nd ed.). Boston, MA: Allyn & Bacon.

54. Robinson (2005). *Justice Blind?*

55. Robinson, Matthew (2002). The case for a "new victimology": Implications for policing (1–16). In Laura Moriarty (ed.), *Police and Victims*. Upper Saddle River, NJ: Prentice-Hall.

2

Theoretical Background: Strain and Anomie Theories

Crime brings together honest men and concentrates them.

—Émile Durkheim, *The Division of Labor in Society* (1893)[1]

Not only is crime normal, as we established in the last chapter, but it is also functional. That is, crime serves a needed function for any society. Émile Durkheim, studying labor, crime, suicide, and other social realities in the late 1800s in France, explained that criminality created solidarity in society by giving people something on which to focus their disdain and displeasure. Thus, punishment of offenders strengthened the *norms* of society—expectations for behavior—by identifying a class of deviants who needed correction and thereby reminded all people of which kinds of behavior were normal and which were abnormal.

Durkheim's notion of *anomie*—commonly defined as a "state of normlessness" or a condition in society whereby norms for behavior are threatened by some large-scale change—was used to explain crime rate variations as well as risks for suicide.[2] Émile Durkheim was also one of the first to recognize that one could never have enough in a modern capitalistic economy: "It is everlastingly repeated that it is man's nature to be eternally dissatisfied, constantly to advance, without relief or rest, toward an indefinite goal. The longing for infinity is daily represented as a mark of moral distinction."[3] As such, Durkheim's work was highly instrumental in the later works of social control theorists as well as other anomie and strain theorists.[4]

Of the literally dozens of theories aimed at explaining why crime occurs, the theories that are most related to the concept of greed as well as our concept of maximization include anomie and strain theories. Anomie and strain theories posit that criminality is due to

- Pressures to achieve at any cost imposed by the American Dream and the relative importance of the economy in our lives.[5]
- Discrepancies in cultural goals and the legitimate means to achieve them and a stressing of goals over means in American society.[6]
- A shared sense of relative deprivation.[7]
- An unlimited desire for wealth in the context of limited means leading to a problem of adjustment.[8]
- Personal states of egoism and selfishness caused by a lack of integration to and regulation by society.[9]
- Frustration that arises from increased wants and desires in the context of globalization and neoliberalism.[10]
- Goal blockage, the loss of valued items, negative emotion, and noxious stimuli.[11]

All anomie and strain theories, to one degree or another, blame crime on the overpowering influence of the economy on our lives. The theories most relevant for economic sources of strain and for our concept of maximization include Robert Merton's structural strain theory, Steven Messner and Richard Rosenfeld's institutional anomie theory, and Richard Cloward and Lloyd Ohlin's differential opportunity theory. Each is reviewed below.

STRUCTURAL STRAIN

Robert Merton's structural strain theory holds that a disjunction between *goals* and *means* is responsible for criminality. Merton states that "culturally defined goals, purposes and interests" compose "a frame of aspirational reference. They are the things 'worth striving for.'"[12] These goals are institutional in that they arise from and are reinforced by social institutions including informal sources of culture goals such as families and schools.[13] The "acceptable modes of reaching out for these goals" are the institutionalized or legitimate *means*. They are "regulations, rooted in the mores or institutions, of allowable procedures for moving toward [cultural objectives]." Certain means are required, some are allowed, others are preferred, while illegitimate means are prohibited. Merton's terms for these, respectively, are *prescriptions, preferences, permissions*, and *proscriptions*.[14]

Structural strain refers to stress on the institutional norms, which "lose their legitimacy and regulatory power" when people have difficulty achieving their goals legally.[15] Strain is not an individual level or psychological phenomenon but is rather a structural reality produced by differential access to legitimate opportunities across society.[16]

This is not to say that individual-level factors are irrelevant in Merton's theory. Eric Baumer asserts that Merton put forth a multilevel theory that holds that "emergent properties of communities shape the value commitments of individuals, which in turn lead to individual differences in deviant behavior."[17] Factors that affect the process of anomie, according to Baumer, include cultural transmission or learning, as well as numerous individual-level factors. Baumer explains that "the likelihood of innovative behavioral responses will be greater among individuals with a relatively weak commitment to normative means for pursuing those goals. . . . If individuals strongly committed to pursuing monetary success goals remain strongly committed to legitimate means, conformity is the likely behavioral outcome. . . . [When] persons committed to pursuing monetary success goals are only weakly committed to institutionalized legitimate means, they are more apt . . . to satisfy the culturally assimilated monetary success goals through innovative behaviors such as instrumental crime."[18]

Further, Baumer claims criminality will be more likely in those individuals "who also feel particularly alienated from legitimate opportunities through which monetary success goals might be achieved, those who lack major commitments to other culturally valued success goals, those who perceive the risk of detection and punishment to be minimal, those who are dissatisfied with their current financial circumstances and those whose deviance conducive value commitments are reinforced by prolonged exposure to others who share similar values."[19]

Instead of individual factors, Robert Merton's theory focuses on the American Dream, which refers to the overriding institutionalized goal in our country. The American Dream means "making it," "winning the game," or achieving independence and wealth. In America, the overriding goal is money . . . "money *signifies* success; it is the *metric* of success."[20] Merton states: "In some large measure, money has been consecrated as a value in itself, over and above its expenditure for articles of consumption or its use for the enhancement of powers. Money is particularly well adapted to become a symbol of prestige. . . . However acquired, fraudulently or institutionally, it can be used to purchase the same goods and services."[21]

Even the rich—who, by definition, have a lot of money—seek more. According to Merton, "In the American Dream there is no final stopping point. The measure of 'monetary success' is conveniently indefinite and relative. At each income level . . . Americans want just about twenty-five percent more (but of course this 'just a bit more' continues to operate once it is obtained)."[22]

Nikos Passas underscores the never-ending pressure inherent in the motives of capitalism toward consumerism and an insatiable drive for *more*: "Regardless of whether people strive for more; due to natural drives or because of cultural encouragement, the point is that market economies cannot perform without lofty aspirations, consumerism, emphasis on material/monetary goals, and competition. All this leads to the pursuit of constantly moving targets and systematic sources of frustration."[23]

Given the constant striving for more wealth, for greater success, Americans are bound to experience what Merton refers to as *strain*.[24] Living in a "culture-bearing society" causes great difficulty for individuals, including strain.[25] Merton developed five modes of individual adaptation to cultural strain, including conformity, innovation, ritualism, retreatism, and rebellion. These adaptations to strain are depicted in table 2.1. Each of the five categories refers to "role behavior in specific types of situations, not to personality . . . types of more or less enduring response, not types of personality organization."[26]

Conformity, "the most common and widely diffused" adaptation, refers to acceptance of both cultural goals, and institutional means to achieve them.[27] Thus, conformity involves acceptance of the culture goals and institutionalized means, thereby defining normal and law-abiding behaviors. Most Americans conform most of the time.[28]

Innovation is used by "the individual [who] has assimilated the cultural emphasis upon the goal without equally internalizing the institutional norms governing ways and means for its attainment."[29] Innovation as adaptation to strain, according to Merton, involves acceptance of the culture goals and rejection of institutionalized means. Thus the adaptation of innovation is responsible for the greatest share of crime (especially street crime among the lower classes). Merton explained: "The greatest pressures toward deviation are exerted upon the lower strata," and he asserted that "specialized areas of vice and crime constitute a 'normal' response to a situation where the cultural emphasis upon pecuniary success has been absorbed, but where there is little access to conventional and legitimate means for becoming successful."[30]

Table 2.1. Merton's Modes of Adaptation to Anomic Strain

Modes of Adaptation	Cultural Goals	Institutional Means
Conformity	Accept	Accept
Innovation	Accept	Reject
Ritualism	Reject	Accept
Retreatism	Reject	Reject
Rebellion	Reject/Replace	Reject/Replace

Source: Merton, Robert (1957). *Social Theory and Social Structure.* Glencoe, IL: The Free Press.

Merton asserts that not only do the poor accept the American Dream, but also that "the avenues available for moving toward this goal are largely limited by the class structure to those of deviant behavior."[31] For both of these reasons, the American Dream does not acknowledge the reality of American institutional organization. Merton explained: "Goals are held to transcend class lines, not to be bounded by them, yet the actual social organization is such that there exist class differentials in accessibility of the goals. In this setting, a cardinal American virtue, 'ambition,' promotes a cardinal American vice, 'deviant behavior.'"[32] Restated, the poor experience amplified strain and thus possess greater motivation to commit antisocial and criminal behavior.

Merton believed that criminality should be more pronounced among the lower classes. Yet, Merton explained that poverty is most criminogenic when combined with limited opportunity and "a commonly shared system of success symbols."[33] Merton noted that even in slums life is "organized" toward success goals associated with the American Dream. That is, everyone wants to achieve the American Dream, even the poor; yet, they are least able to achieve it given less access to it.[34]

The significant point for this book is that the American Dream is thus a universal value—one focused on pecuniary gain. While money is not the only goal associated with America, it is a significant one to be sure.[35] Merton does not assert that everyone aspires to the "same concrete goals of success . . . that everyone can be a multi-millionaire, everyone can be a success." Instead, he claims that everyone is taught "to the point that it [is] 'taken for granted,' that the USA offer[s] 'limitless possibilities' to all. . . . The core cultural message [is] that it [is] *legitimate* for all members of American society to pursue and expect economic success. Social ascent—upward universal social mobility—[is] universally prescribed."[36]

None of this should be taken to mean that Merton's theory was limited to street crime, although that is how it has historically been applied. Merton never thought of his theory as limited to crime committed by the poor. As noted in a published interview, Robert Merton said his theory was "not at all limited to the lower reaches of the social structure. . . . Within each domain, the same processes may be at work but produce different kinds of deviant behavior because it is a different world."[37] An additional quote from Merton says it best: "Fraud, corruption, vice, crime, in short, the entire catalogue of proscribed behavior, becomes increasingly common when the emphasis on the *culturally induced success-goal* becomes divorced from a coordinated institutional emphasis."[38]

No matter how much one obtains, it is always possible to want more; further, it is possible to feel deprived relative to others who have more than you. This is the assumption underlying the concept of *relative deprivation*.

Relative deprivation is an important concept to understand, for it can be used to explain acts of deviance and criminality by even the very wealthy. Craig Weber explains that what is key to understanding relative deprivation is the distinction between *expectation* and *aspiration*: "If we *expect* something to happen we are likely to feel discontented if it does not materialize. If we *aspire* to something then we may feel less discontent if it does not materialize.[39] Thus, even wealthy people who expect to achieve more can experience a form of strain when they do not.

So too can anyone living in America's consumeristic economy. According to Weber, the "modern consumer experience" can be described as a form of relative deprivation "engendered by the creation of markets where demand is unfulfilled by supply. . . . The frustration of not having next year's electronic gadget today has become normalized, whether or not it is the frustration of anticipation or the anticipation of frustration. . . . The normalization of frantic consumerism, the transformation of wants into needs, means that relative deprivation is an integral part of consumerism."[40] If true, strain ought to be common in U.S. society, which is highly consumeristic. Further, adaptation to stain through maximization also ought to be common.

Ritualism "involves the abandoning or scaling down of the lofty cultural goals of great pecuniary success and rapid social mobility to the point where one's aspirations can be satisfied." Ritualism involves rejecting the cultural goal of self-advancement, "to get ahead in the world," while simultaneously abiding "almost compulsively by institutional norms."[41] That is, ritualism embodies the rejection of culture goals, yet concomitantly an acceptance of institutionalized means. Those engaged in this adaptation to strain continue to work and abide by the rules of the game without being interested in winning it.

Retreatism, the least common adaptation according to Merton, involves a rejection of both the goals of the culture and the institutionalized means to achieve them. Those engaged in retreatism are in essence "*in* society but not *of* it." In this category are "some of the adaptive activities of psychotics, autists, pariahs, outcasts, vagrants, vagabonds, tramps, chronic drunkards and drug addicts."[42]

Merton asserts that retreatism occurs when people have accepted both the goals and the means of society but have not succeeded through accessible institutionalized means: "The competitive order is maintained by the frustrated and handicapped individual who cannot cope with this order and drops out. Defeatism, quietism and resignation are manifested in escape mechanisms which ultimately lead him to 'escape' from the requirements of the society."[43] Merton thus described retreatism as an adaptation of self-destructive and maladaptive types of behaviors.

Rebellion, Merton's final adaptation to strain, also involves rejection of both the culture goals and the institutionalized means, but those who pursue rebellion develop their own substitute goals and means that often conflict with those endorsed by societal institutions such as the family and schools. Rebellion leads people to "bring into being a new . . . greatly modified social structure," one where "the standards of success would be sharply modified and provision would be made for a closer correspondence between merit, effort and reward."[44] Prior to rebellion, one of two things must occur. Either, (1) alienation from goals and means occurs, both of which become seen as "purely arbitrary," and/or (2) "transvaluation" occurs, "where the direct or vicarious experience of frustration leads to full denunciation of previously prized values."[45]

According to Merton, the American Dream produces deviance and criminality in ways besides goals–means discrepancies. For example, when discussing the robber barons of the late nineteenth century, Merton points out that the "cultural structure in which the sacrosanct goal virtually consecrates the means" led Americans to "reluctant admiration" of this goal, and hence, to the foundation of the American Dream.

When discussing a hypothetical malintegrated culture, Merton explained it is possible that culturally prescribed goals may overcome and completely dominate consideration of culturally prescribed means: "There may develop a very heavy, at times virtually exclusive, stress upon the value of particular goals, involving comparatively little concern with the institutionally prescribed means of striving toward these goals."[46] American institutions of the 1950s, according to Merton, placed greater emphasis on culture goals than upon institutional or legitimate means to achieve them. This resulted in an overwhelming focus on the cultural goals of American institutions with relatively little emphasis on the institutionalized means.

When emphasis on institutionalized means relaxes and goals are overemphasized, the result may be anomie and criminality. Thus, the goal of pursuing success can encourage people to commit crime. As Merton wrote, "an extreme cultural emphasis on the goal of success attenuates conformity to institutionally prescribed methods of moving toward this goal."[47] Therefore, the American Dream itself may be viewed as criminogenic.

Essentially, Merton asserted that our focus on the American Dream is too strong, stating the "emphasis on the goal has so attenuated the satisfactions deriving from sheer participation in the competitive activity that only a successful outcome provides gratification."[48] In other words, "winning" or "making it" according to the rules becomes secondary to "winning" or "making it" by *any means necessary*. The American Dream, by emphasizing individualism and materialism, "encourages people to adopt an 'anything goes' mentality in the pursuit of personal goals."[49] Although Merton did not specifically discuss the implementation of both legitimate and illegitimate means (maximization), it is clear, that for some, incorporation of this multivariate adaptation to strain justifies deviance and/or criminality, as long as it is in pursuit of the American Dream.

Anomie can also occur at the individual level. At the individual level, *microanomie* refers to a cognitive state "where self-enhancing values are higher priority than self-transcending values." This occurs when "an individual is not regulated by values that call for behavior aligned more with social than self interests. When an individual's value orientation is skewed toward self, he or she is in effect unregulated by social interests and therefore inclined to act against them. This condition . . . is more likely to produce criminal behavior."[50]

Contained within the mantra of the American Dream is the ethos that success results from "personal" strengths, that is, from hard work and determination of people with strong wills. Thus, failure in the United States is generally perceived as a "personal" failure rather than a systemic flaw.[51] Assuming all failures are personal/moral failures rather than system failures, the threat or fear of defeat may serve to motivate people to succeed, to attain the American Dream, by any and all means necessary. As Merton wrote: "The moral mandate to achieve success . . . exerts pressure to succeed, by fair means if possible and by foul means if necessary."[52] One possible accommodation to strain is rejection of institutionalized means and replacement with deviant or illegitimate means to achieve the proscribed goals (innovation). Others might simply keep playing the game (ritualism), give up and withdraw (retreatism), or develop new goals that are easier for them to achieve and live with (rebellion).

Merton declares that quitting is the only option that is not acceptable in America: "Americans are admonished 'not to be a quitter' for in the dictionary of American culture, as in the lexicon of youth, 'there is no such word as fail.' The cultural manifesto is clear; one must not quit, must not cease striving, must not lessen his goals, for 'not failure, but low aim, is crime.'"[53] Merton also states that the American Dream emphasizes "penalizing . . . those who draw in their ambitions."[54] Although Merton did not specifically discuss the issue, it follows from Merton's logic that those who commit deviant and criminal acts after quitting or giving up may be judged more harshly by society than those who commit such acts in the context of legitimate means (such as work) that are used to pursue wealth.

Merton's declinations give us the sense he recognized that crime is normal and to be expected given the prevalence of messages related to pursuing the American Dream, which he describes as a *moral obligation* to pursue.[55] If we assume that Americans have generally accepted the American Dream and are deeply committed to it, a logical inference would be that when people pursue the American Dream through illegal or deviant means, others will react to them less harshly than if they commit crime in pursuit of goals unrelated to the American Dream given that the "criminal" is simply pursuing a moral obligation.

INSTITUTIONAL ANOMIE

Steven Messner and Richard Rosenfeld also attribute high crime rates in the United States to our allegiance to the American Dream. These authors define the American Dream as the "broad cultural ethos that entails a commitment to *the goal of material success*, to be pursued by everyone in society, under conditions of open, individual competition."[56] It can be better understood in terms of four values—achievement, individualism, universalism, and the "fetishism of money."[57] Achievement refers to making something of oneself whereby "the failure to achieve is readily equated with a failure to make any meaningful contribution to society."[58] Individualism refers to the status of one person above society whereby people are "encouraged to make it on their own" by, if necessary, disregarding normative restraints on behavior.[59] Universalism refers to the fact that everyone is encouraged to pursue the American Dream. Finally, the fetishism of money refers to the "preeminent role of money as the 'metric' of success."[60]

Part of the problem with the American Dream, according to Messner and Rosenfeld, is *cultural* (whereby messages inherent in the American Dream create criminal motivations through innovation and anomie) and part of the problem is *structural* (whereby the economy dominates other societal institutions). The cultural argument asserts that American culture is characterized by a strong emphasis on the goal of monetary success and a weak emphasis on the importance of the legitimate means for the pursuit of success. The combination of strong pressures to succeed monetarily and weak restraints on the selection of means is intrinsic to the dominant cultural ethos of the American Dream. The American Dream contributes to crime directly by encouraging people to employ illegal means to achieve goals that are culturally approved.[61]

Like Merton, Messner and Rosenfeld agree that the American Dream "encourages an exaggerated emphasis on monetary achievement while devaluing alternative criterion of success, it promotes a preoccupation with the realization of goals while de-emphasizing the importance of the ways in which these goals are pursued."[62] According to Jon Bernburg, the American Dream thus "creates pressure to achieve, but minimizes the pressure to play by the rules. Under these circumstances, people become more likely to use the 'most technically efficient means necessary' in reaching their goals. The result is a higher rate of predatory crime."[63]

In some cases, the cultural emphasis on achievement, which promotes productivity and innovation, also generates pressures to succeed at any cost.[64] Stated simply, "In the 'rush to get ahead,' it is sometimes necessary to 'find an edge,' 'cut a corner,' bend 'principle to circumstance,' 'cheat a little,' 'lie a little.'"[65] The use of violent means to achieve or regain control in underworld markets, like the use of illegal nonviolent means (such as price fixing or insider trading) to control legitimate markets, receives strong, if indirect, cultural support in our society.[66]

Institutional anomie theory builds on Merton's ideas to point out that less *and* more opportunity can lead to criminality. Frustration related to not being able to legally meet one's goals due to less opportunity is commonly called "strain." Institutional anomie theory adds that "an expansion of economic opportunities, rather than lessening the level of anomie in society, may actually intensify culturally induced pressures to use extralegal means to acquire monetary rewards."[67] Why does this happen? Messner and Rosenfeld assert that people are socialized to accept the desirability of pursuing the goal of material success, and they are encouraged to believe that the chances of realizing the American Dream are sufficiently high to justify a continued commitment to this cultural goal. Further, the imperative to succeed, or at least to keep on trying to succeed, respects no social boundaries.[68]

One outcome of the universal nature of the American Dream is that it inevitably creates not only alienation (for those unable to achieve the dream), but also maintains inequality.[69] As explained by Messner and Rosenfeld: "Despite the universalistic component of the American Dream, the basic logic of this cultural ethos actually *presupposes* high levels of inequality. A competitive allocation of monetary rewards requires both winners and losers, and winning and losing have meaning only when rewards are distributed unequally. The motivation to endure the competitive struggle is not maintained easily if the monetary difference between winning and losing is inconsequential.[70]

Economic inequality has been remarkably stagnant in American society. "The poorest fifth of families and unattached individuals have consistently received about between 4 and 5 percent and the richest fifth, between 40 and 45 percent of total income for over a half century.... The richest 1 percent of the U.S. population has owned somewhere between 20 and 36 percent of all assets in American since 1820."[71] This, too, is another source of criminality in the United States.[72]

As for the structural part of the argument, Messner and Rosenfeld state that the American Dream also exerts an indirect effect on crime through its interconnections with the institutional balance of power in society.[73] Messner and Rosenfeld identify significant institutions in American society—the economy, polity, family, and education—and claim that the economy is the most important of the group. The economy refers to "activities organized around the production and distribution of goods and services." The polity refers to the political system, which "mobilizes and distributes power to attain collective goals." The family raises and socializes children "into the values, goals, and beliefs of the dominant culture." Finally, education is responsible for "preparing youth for the demands of adult roles and, in particular, occupational roles."[74]

According to Messner and Rosenfeld, in order for society to function appropriately, these four institutions must be coordinated and cooperate. However, America's most cherished values—"a strong achievement orientation, a commitment to competitive individualism, universalism, and, most important, the glorification of material success"—are rooted in economic concerns. Further, the other social institutions are unable to "tame economic imperatives."[75] This occurs in three ways:

1. *Devaluation of noneconomic institutional functions and roles*—for example, those who perform family-oriented tasks such as childcare are paid very little in the United States; educational pursuits are often reduced to the relevance they have for assisting one with earning money and with career advancement; people see the primary purpose of government as encouraging and assisting with economic growth.
2. *Accommodation to economic requirements by other social institutions*—for example, families often must make serious sacrifices in terms of time spent together so that both parents can work full time; students in public schools are encouraged to raise money for their schools by selling products for corporations whereby a portion is donated to the school; politicians depend on donations by lobbyists for major corporations, wealthy individuals, and political action committees to raise enough money to compete in and win elections.
3. *Penetration of economic norms into other institutional domains*—for example, a bottom-line, businesslike mentality is utilized in families, schools, and lawmaking activities in much of what they do.[76]

Since the "primary task for noneconomic institutions such as the family and schools is to inculcate beliefs, values, and commitments other than those of the marketplace, we should not expect these types of situations to control antisocial and criminal behaviors when they are weakened.[77] The adaptations delineated within the framework of *institutional anomie* theory suggest that "when other institutions such as polity, religion, education, and the family are unable to regulate human impulses generated by the economy, criminality and deviance are more likely."[78]

Stated differently, when "the social organization of the United States is characterized by a striking dominance of the economy in the institutional balance of power . . . the inherent tendencies of a capitalist economy to orient the members of society toward an unrestrained pursuit of economic achievements are developed to an extreme degree. These tendencies are expressed at the cultural level in the preeminence of the competitive, individualistic pursuit of monetary success as the overriding goal—the American Dream—and in the relative deemphasis placed on the importance of using normative means to reach this goal—anomie. The anomic nature of the American Dream and the institutional structure of American society are thus mutually supportive and reinforcing."[79]

In their book *The War Against Parents*, Sylvia Hewlett and Cornell West show how society has abandoned parents. Their main claim is that parents have been hurt by managerial greed, as well as government tax, housing policies, and our media culture. They assert that market work centered on profit and motivated by greed "crowds out" nonmarket work (which is centered on commitment and care). Further, the authors underscore how some products aimed at making it easier for parents actually strain good parenting while simultaneously earning corporations very large profits (e.g., fast food, soda, sweetened juices and cereals).[80] This is illustrative of how the economy dominates or takes precedence over the family.

Jon Bernburg states that criminal behavior is most likely when "the value-orientation of the market economy, that is, the pursuit of self-interest, attraction to monetary rewards, and competition, become exaggerated relative to the value-orientations of institutions such as the family, education, and the polity."[81] A study by Mitchell Chamlin and John Cochran seems to confirm this. When noneconomic institutions such as the family, schools, and polity are strong, the effects of economic pressure on both property crimes and violent crimes are weaker.[82] Further, an international study of homicide rates found countries that protect their citizens from economic intrusions and income inequality through social welfare policies have less crime. These findings indicate that lethal violence is most robust in societies that do not protect their citizens from the deleterious effects of inequality.[83] The theory has been supported in other studies, including the effects of noneconomic institutions as well as instrumental and expressive homicides.[84] Thus, research appears to support this theoretical perspective and suggests that the American Dream is criminogenic.[85]

Scholar David Simon illustrates how the welfare of the economy in America often interferes with quality of life for U.S. citizens: "The United States remains the only advanced industrial democracy without paid family leave, without national health care, without an extended family vacation policy precisely because the needs of business are given precedence over everything else in the American institutional order."[86] A recent study found that the United States ranked dead last in providing timely and effective health care to its citizens, something that has been linked to reductions in premature and preventable deaths. The result of placing last rather than in the top three nations? Roughly 101,000 additional deaths per year.[87]

One problem with institutional anomie theory is that it is not directly testable; instead, it has been assessed indirectly by examining the impact of various economic variables on crime rates.[88] Some research calls into question the assumption of institutional anomie theory that Americans value money above other institutions such as the family. For example, Gary Jensen found that the United States is tied for second among thirty-four nations in terms of the importance of the family, fifth for the importance of religion, tied for ninth for the importance of leisure, and tied for fifteenth for the importance of work. According to Jensen, this suggests that Americans "are quite distinctive among industrialized nations in the importance accorded the family and religion in their lives."[89]

Jensen also found that more than 70 percent of Americans agree that "less emphasis on money and material possessions would be a good thing" suggesting to him that "Americans do not appear particularly materialistic relative to other industrialized nations."[90] We believe Jensen's conclusion is not warranted. That a large majority of Americans say that "less emphasis on money and material possessions would be a good thing" suggests to us that there *is* too much emphasis placed on money in American society. These findings merely suggest that Americans are aware of this fact.

Further, when Americans respond to questions asking them how important their families are, there is a significant possibility that they are responding to the question in a way they think they are supposed to respond—a *social desirability effect*. A better measure would be behavioral—what Americans actually do. A citizen working full time works forty hours a week—roughly 8 am to 5 pm, Monday through Friday. When you add in travel time to and from work, time to cook and clean, walk the dog, change the cat box, and so forth, where is the time to spend with children in family contexts? Studies show that American children spend about four hours a day watching television and/or playing video games, but less than twenty minutes a day with their parents in meaningful conversations or activities.[91]

There are also measures available that show how little the family is valued in the context of work in America. For example, Stephanie Coontz writes that "107 other countries in the world protect working women's right to breast-feed on the job; 137 countries mandate paid annual leave, with 121 of these countries guaranteeing two weeks or more each year; 134 have laws that fix the maximum length of the work week; 49 guaranteeing leave for major family events, such as marriages or funerals; and 145 countries provide paid leave for short- or long-term illnesses. The United States does not offer any of these guarantees."[92] Clearly, work takes precedence over everything else for most Americans.

Mitchell Chamlin and John Cochran utilized questions from the World Values Survey to assess whether Americans embrace money more so than citizens in other nations. They did this by assessing what portion of Americans and citizens from other countries say that a good income is the most important attribute of gainful employment and what portion say placing less emphasis on money and material possessions would be a good thing. Chamlin and Cochran found that nearly a third of Americans say that money is the most important reason to go to work, and that about 60 percent of other nations return higher percentages to this question than the United States. Further, nearly 70 percent of Americans say that less emphasis on money and material possessions would be a good thing, and only three other nations had a higher portion of citizens indicate this sentiment.[93]

Chamlin and Cochran conclude: "The results are clear. When compared to a larger and more heterogeneous (with respect of economic development) sample of countries, we find no evidence in support of Messner and Rosenfeld's core assumption that American culture places an unparalleled emphasis on the acquisition of goods and services."[94] We believe Chamlin and Cochran's conclusion is incorrect. That a higher portion of citizens in only three nations say that less emphasis on money and material possessions would be a good thing suggests to us that there is in fact too much emphasis placed on money in American society. Like Jensen's study, Chamlin and Cochran's findings merely suggest Americans are aware of this. The problem with Chamlin and Cochran's conclusion is that it is not exclusive—other possible interpretations are available.

DIFFERENTIAL OPPORTUNITY

Richard Cloward and Lloyd Ohlin concur with Merton's central thesis concerning strain. They discuss how humanity's desire for wealth is virtually unlimited and wrote: "There is every reason to think that persons variously located in the social hierarchy have rather different chances of reaching common success-goals despite the prevailing ideology of equal opportunity."[95] The variants of success in pursuit of the American Dream lead to feelings of strain in individuals, or what Cloward and Ohlin called "a major problem of adjustment."

Cloward and Ohlin then applied Robert Merton's basic ideas to individual subcultures—smaller groups within cultures, or cultures within cultures— that share values and norms differing from and often conflicting with those of the larger culture. Strain can not only lead to criminality among individuals, but can also lead to shared feelings of oppression and thus a subculture: "The disparity between what lower-class youth are led to want and what is actually available to them is the source of a major problem of adjustment. Adolescents who form delinquent subcultures . . . have internalized an emphasis upon conventional goals. Faced with limitations on legitimate avenues of access to these goals, and unable to revise their aspirations downward, they experience intense frustrations; the exploration of nonconformist alternatives may be the result."

Some barriers to success discussed by Cloward and Ohlin include educational, cultural, and economic obstacles that lead to incorporation of illegitimate means of opportunity.

When strain becomes a "common perception" and when members share a "sense of indignation about their disadvantages" normal interaction "may provide encouragement for the withdrawal of sentiment in support of the established system of norms. Once freed of allegiance to the existing set of rules, such persons may devise or adopt delinquent means of achieving success."[96] New norm systems replace traditional systems of norms in different kinds of subcultures.

In studying adolescent male delinquent gangs in large, lower-class, urban areas, Cloward and Ohlin discovered three types of subcultures. First, the *criminal subculture* is "a type of gang which is devoted to theft, extortion, and other illegal means of securing income." Second, the *conflict subculture* is "a type of gang in which the manipulation of violence predominates as a way of winning status." Third, the *retreatist subculture* is "a type of gang in which the consumption of drugs is stressed."[97]

According to the theory of differential opportunity, the type of delinquent subculture that develops in a particular area depends upon several factors, including the (1) neighborhood milieu as relates to social organization, (2) nature of role models for gang members, (3) age levels of offenders (whether older, experienced criminal role models are present), (4) bonds between criminal and conventional elements, and (5) other factors that affect opportunities for criminal behavior. Cloward and Ohlin explain: "If, in a given social location, illegal or criminal means are not readily available, then we should not expect a criminal subculture to develop among adolescents. By the same logic, we should expect the manipulation of violence to become a primary avenue to higher status only in areas where the means of violence are not denied to the young. . . . Drug addiction and participation in subcultures organized around the consumption of drugs presuppose that persons can secure access to drugs and knowledge about how to use them. In some parts of the social structure, this would be very difficult; in others, very easy. In short, there are marked differences from one part of the social structure to another in the types of illegitimate adaptation that are available to persons in search of solutions to problems of adjustment arising from the restricted availability of legitimate means."[98]

Cloward and Ohlin were among the first to explicitly state that both legitimate and illegitimate opportunities can vary among people and places, hence the term *differential opportunity*. Merton too used the phrase "differential opportunity structures" to describe how people's access to legitimate means of success was determined by society.[99]

Other anomie and strain theories were incomplete, Cloward and Ohlin argued, because they ignored "the *relative availability* of illegal alternatives to various potential criminals. The aspiration to be a physician is hardly enough to explain the fact of becoming a physician; there is much that transpires between the aspiration and the achievement. This is no less true of the person who wants to be a successful criminal."[100] Just as there is a differential distribution of legitimate means, there also is a differential distribution of illegitimate means.

In sum, Cloward and Ohlin delineate the reality that an innovator needs to learn the skills of and have opportunities for illegitimate behavior just as the conformist needs to learn the skills requisite in and have opportunities for the socially acceptable pursuit of the American Dream. It seems logical that for many individuals, groups, types of occupational roles, and subcultures opportunities will exist for both legitimate and illegitimate behaviors, or conformity and innovation. It is also possible that people can utilize these modes of adaptation simultaneously.

THE MAXIMIZER

When one explicitly considers illegitimate means in pursuit of the American Dream, a new adaptation to strain emerges. Table 2.2 depicts this new mode of adaptation and illustrates that Robert Merton's five modes of adaptation are left intact. Since we have already defined those modes of adaptation, we will only focus here on the one we have added—the maximizer. Note that we have added a third column to Merton's typology. The new column represents acceptance or rejection of illegitimate means (i.e., criminality) in pursuit of one's goals.

Table 2.2. Merton's Modes of Adaptation to Anomic Strain, Expanded to Include Noninstitutionalized Means

Modes of Adaptation	Cultural Goals	Institutional Means	Criminality
Conformity	Accept	Accept	Reject
Innovation	Accept	Reject	Accept
Ritualism	Reject	Accept	Reject
Retreatism	Reject	Reject	Accept
Rebellion	Reject/Replace	Reject/Replace	Accept
Maximization	Accept	Accept	Accept

Those involved in maximization, like those involved in conformity, accept culture goals and therefore are in pursuit of the American Dream. The difference is that those who utilize strategies of conformity pursue legitimate or institutionalized means to achieve their goals of "making it" or "winning" the game, whereas those who utilize strategies of maximization pursue legitimate or institutionalized means, as well as illegitimate or noninstutitionalized means in pursuit of culture goals. Thus, maximization involves a combination of conformity and innovation. Maximization, we believe, refers to a role behavior that emerges in specific types of situations and that it is a form of enduring response to strain found in those specific types of situations.

An example of maximization might better illustrate its meaning. A building contractor involved in legitimate business is, by definition, using legitimate or institutionalized means in pursuit of the American Dream. This is conformity. Those contractors who also regularly accept norms that allow criminal behavior as part of the job and thus commit deviant acts and/or break the law (i.e., innovation) to achieve even greater profit/wealth would be characterized as *maximizers*. The maximizer is one who utilizes both legitimate and illegitimate means in pursuit of the American Dream. He or she must have the knowledge, skills, and opportunities necessary to engage in a legal trade, as well the knowledge, skills, and opportunities necessary to successfully commit criminal behavior aimed at maximizing the American Dream.

In the next chapter, we lay out a new theory of crime organized around the concept of maximization, a theory we call *contextual anomie/strain theory*. The main premise of the theory is similar to that of anomie and strain theories—the American Dream promotes criminality through greed, strain, and anomie. Whereas everyone is subjected to the pressures of the American Dream, we add that it is more pronounced in certain contexts of society (e.g., the corporate subculture). That is, in American corporations, there are added pressures to engage in innovation simultaneously to conformity so that criminality in the context of work is now viewed as quite normal.

NOTES

1. Durkheim, Émile (1893). *The Division of Labor in Society*. Translated by George Simpson. New York: The Free Press.

2. Durkheim, Émile (1897). *Suicide*. New York: The Free Press.

3. Durkheim, Émile (1897, 1966). *Suicide*. New York: The Free Press, 257.

4. Vold, George, Thomas Bernard, and Jeffrey Snipes (2001). *Theoretical Criminology* (5th ed.). New York: Oxford University Press.

5. Messner, Steven, and Richard Rosenfeld (1994). *Crime and the American Dream*. New York: Wadsworth.

6. Merton, Robert (1957). *Social Theory and Social Structure*. Glencoe, IL: The Free Press.

7. Pratt, Travis, and Timothy Godsey (2003). Social support, inequality, and homicide: A cross-national test of an integrated theoretical model. *Criminology* 41: 611–43.

8. Cloward, Richard, and Lloyd Ohlin (1961). *Delinquency and Opportunity: A Theory of Delinquent Gangs*. New York: The Free Press.

9. Konty, Mark (2005). Microanomie: The cognitive foundations of the relationship between anomie and deviance. *Criminology* 43: 107–31.

10. Passas, Nikos (2000). Global anomie, dysnomie, and economic crime: Hidden consequences of neoliberalism and globalization in Russia and around the world. *Social Justice* 27: 16–44.

11. Agnew, Robert (1992). Foundation for a general strain theory of crime and delinquency. *Criminology* 30: 47–87; Agnew, Robert (1999). A general strain theory of community differences in crime rates. *The Journal of Research in Crime and Delinquency* 36: 123–55; Agnew, Robert (2002). Experienced, vicarious, and anticipated strain: An exploratory study on physical victimization and delinquency. *Justice Quarterly* 19: 603–32; Agnew, Robert, Timothy Brezina, John Wright, and Francis Cullen (2002). Strain, personality traits, and delinquency: Extending general strain theory. *Criminology* 40: 43–71.

12. Merton, *Social Theory and Social Structure*, 132.

13. Merton, *Social Theory and Social Structure*, 137.

14. Merton, *Social Theory and Social Structure,* 132.

15. Cullen, Francis, and Steven Messner (2007). The making of criminology revisited: An oral history of Merton's anomie paradigm. *Theoretical Criminology* 11(1): 11.

16. Cullen and Messner, The making of criminology revisited, 21.

17. Baumer, Eric (2007). Untangling research puzzles in Merton's multilevel theory. *Theoretical Criminology* 11(1): 66.

18. Baumer, Untangling research puzzles, 73.

19. Baumer, Untangling research puzzles, 77.

20. Messner, Steven (2003). An institutional-anomie theory of crime: Continuities and elaborations in the study of social structure and anomie. *Cologne Journal of Sociology and Social Psychology* 43(1): 98–99.

21. Merton, *Social Theory and Social Structure,* 136.

22. Merton, *Social Theory and Social Structure*, 136.

23. Passas, Nikos (2000). Global anomie, dysnomie, and economic crime: Hidden consequences of neoliberalism and globalization in Russia and around the world. *Social Justice* 27: 19.

24. Merton, *Social Theory and Social Structure*, 139.

25. Merton, *Social Theory and Social Structure*, 139.

26. Merton, *Social Theory and Social Structure*, 140.

27. Merton, *Social Theory and Social Structure*, 141.

28. Matza, David (1964). *Delinquency and Drift*. New York: John Wiley & Sons.

29. Merton, *Social Theory and Social Structure*, 141.

30. Merton, *Social Theory and Social Structure*, 141.

31. Merton, *Social Theory and Social Structure*, 144–45.

32. Merton, *Social Theory and Social Structure*, 146.

33. Cullen and Messner, The making of criminology revisited, 25.

34. Cullen and Messner, The making of criminology revisited, 16.

35. Cullen and Messner, The making of criminology revisited, 23.

36. Cullen and Messner, The making of criminology revisited, 24.

37. Cullen and Messner, The making of criminology revisited, 30.

38. Merton, Robert (1938). Social structure and anomie. *American Sociological Review* 3: 676–77.

39. Weber, Craig (2007). Reevaluating relative deprivation theory. *Theoretical Criminology* 11(1): 99.

40. Weber, Reevaluating relative deprivation theory, 113.

41. Merton, *Social Theory and Social Structure*, 149–50.

42. Merton, *Social Theory and Social Structure*, 153.

43. Merton, *Social Theory and Social Structure*, 153.

44. Merton, *Social Theory and Social Structure*, 155.

45. Merton, *Social Theory and Social Structure*, 156.

46. Merton, *Social Theory and Social Structure*, 132.

47. Merton, *Social Theory and Social Structure*, 169.

48. Merton, *Social Theory and Social Structure*, 135.

49. Chamlin, Mitchell, and John Cochran (2007). An evaluation of the assumptions that underlie institutional anomie theory. *Theoretical Criminology* 11(1): 45.

50. Konty, Mark (2005). Microanomie: The cognitive foundations of the relationship between anomie and deviance. *Criminology* 43: 107.

51. Merton, *Social Theory and Social Structure*, 138.

52. Merton, *Social Theory and Social Structure*, 169.

53. Merton, *Social Theory and Social Structure*, 139.

54. Merton, *Social Theory and Social Structure*, 138.

55. Merton, *Social Theory and Social Structure*, 168.

56. Messner, Steven, and Richard Rosenfeld (1994). *Crime and the American Dream*. New York: Wadsworth, 6. [Emphasis added.]

57. Messner and Rosenfeld, *Crime and the American Dream*, 62–63.

58. Messner and Rosenfeld, *Crime and the American Dream*, 62.

59. Messner and Rosenfeld, *Crime and the American Dream*, 63.

60. Messner and Rosenfeld, *Crime and the American Dream*, 63.

61. Messner and Rosenfeld, *Crime and the American Dream*, ix.

62. Messner and Rosenfeld, *Crime and the American Dream*, 10.

63. Bernburg, Jon (2002). Anomie, social change and crime. *The British Journal of Criminology* 42: 732.

64. Messner and Rosenfeld, *Crime and the American Dream*, 7.

65. Messner and Rosenfeld, *Crime and the American Dream*, 61.

66. Messner and Rosenfeld, *Crime and the American Dream*, 3.

67. Chamlin and Cochran, An evaluation of the assumptions, 40.

68. Messner and Rosenfeld, *Crime and the American Dream*, 6–8.

69. Messner and Rosenfeld, *Crime and the American Dream*, 8–9.

70. Messner and Rosenfeld, *Crime and the American Dream*, 9.

71. Messner and Rosenfeld, *Crime and the American Dream*, 9.

72. Robinson, Matthew (2004). *Why Crime? An Integrated Systems Theory of Antisocial Behavior.* Upper Saddle River, NJ: Prentice Hall.

73. Messner and Rosenfeld, *Crime and the American Dream*, ix.

74. Messner and Rosenfeld, *Crime and the American Dream*, 65–66.

75. Messner and Rosenfeld, *Crime and the American Dream*, 68.

76. Maume, Michael, and Matthew Lee (2003). Social institutions and violence: A sub-national test of Institutional Anomie Theory. *Criminology* 41: 1140; Savolainen, Jukka (2000). Inequality, welfare state, and homicide: Further support for the Institutional Anomie Theory. *Criminology* 38: 1022.

77. Messner and Rosenfeld, *Crime and the American Dream*, 10.

78. Robinson, *Why Crime?*, 227; citing Chamlin, Mitchell, and John Cochran (1995). Assessing Messner and Rosenfeld's Institutional Anomie Theory: A partial test. *Criminology* 33: 411–29.

79. Messner and Rosenfeld, *Crime and the American Dream*, 76.

80. Hewlett, Sylvia, and Cornell West (1998). *The War Against Parents.* Boston, MA: Houghton Mifflin.

81. Bernburg, Anomie, social change and crime, 729–42.

82. Chamlin and Cochran, Assessing Messner and Rosenfeld's Institutional Anomie Theory, 411–29.

83. Savolainen, Inequality, welfare state, and homicide, 1021–42.

84. Maume and Lee, Social institutions and violence, 1137–72.

85. Piquero, Alex, and Nicole Piquero (1998). On testing institutional anomie theory with varying specifications. *Studies on Crime & Crime Prevention* 7: 61–84.

86. Simon, David (2006). *Elite Deviance* (8th ed.). Boston, MA: Allyn and Bacon, 286.

87. Yahoo News (2008). France is health care leader, US comes dead last: Study. Retrieved January 8, 2008, from news.yahoo.com/s/afp/20080108/lf_afp/ushealth-francemortality_080108191353.

88. Chamlin and Cochran, An evaluation of the assumptions, 41.

89. Jensen, Gary (2002). Institutional anomie theory and social variations in crime: A critical appraisal. *International Journal of Sociology and Social Policy* 22(7/8): 58–59.

90. Jensen, Institutional anomie theory and social variations in crime, 60.

91. For example, see Amato, Paul, Alan Booth, David Johnson, and Stacy Rogers (2007). *Alone Together: How Marriage in America Is Changing.* Cambridge, MA: Harvard University Press.

92. Coontz, Stephanie (2007). The family revolution. *Greater Good* Fall: 15.

93. Chamlin and Cochran, An evaluation of the assumptions, 51–53.

94. Chamlin and Cochran, An evaluation of the assumptions, 53.

95. Cloward, Richard, and Lloyd Ohlin (1961). *Delinquency and Opportunity: A Theory of Delinquent Gangs.* New York: The Free Press, 85.

96. Cloward and Ohlin, *Delinquency and Opportunity*, 108–9.

97. Cloward and Ohlin, *Delinquency and Opportunity*, 1.

98. Cloward and Ohlin, *Delinquency and Opportunity*, 151–52.

99. Cullen and Messner, The making of criminology revisited, 11.

100. Cloward and Ohlin, *Delinquency and Opportunity*, 145.

3

Contextual Anomie/Strain Theory

A sizable fraction of inner-city young men engage in both legal and illegal
activity at the same time, moving back and forth from one to the other as
opportunity permits.

—Steven Messner and Richard Rosenfeld,
Crime and the American Dream (2001)[1]

Research has discovered that street criminals take advantage of legitimate
and illegitimate means available to them in order to "get ahead." Further,
David Matza's theory of "delinquency and drift" long ago demonstrated that
juvenile offenders often drift in and out of delinquency and conformity, in
part due to guilt associated with wrongful behavior.[2] This might lead you to
believe that our concept of maximization—simultaneously abiding by the
law (conformity) and breaking it (innovation)—has already been written
about in a substantial way, but this is not the case. Maximization has never
been explicitly acknowledged in the literature. While others have identified
the reality that criminals moved back and forth between conformity and innovation, our assertion is that people in given situations engage in conformity
and innovation simultaneously—that the boundaries between the two often
become blurred and even irrelevant.

As we showed in the last chapter, no anomie and strain theorist has considered other ways to adapt to strains associated with living in America's
anomic society. When one explicitly considers illegitimate means in pursuit
of the American Dream, a new adaptation to strain emerges. The mode of
adaptation to strain we added is called maximization. Those involved in
maximization, like those involved in conformity, accept culture goals and
therefore are in pursuit of the American Dream. The difference is that those

who utilize strategies of conformity pursue legitimate or institutionalized means to achieve their goals of "making it" or "winning" the game, whereas those who utilize strategies of maximization pursue legitimate or institutionalized means, as well as illegitimate or noninstututionalized means in pursuit of culture goals. Thus, maximization involves a combination of conformity and innovation. Maximization, we believe, refers to a role behavior that emerges in specific types of situations and that it is a form of enduring response to strain found in those specific types of situations.

In this chapter, we lay out our new theory of criminality—*contextual anomie/strain theory*—and explain how maximization is the most significant part of the theory. Then, in chapters 4 and 5, we apply the concept of maximization to corporate crime.

CONTEXTUAL ANOMIE/STRAIN THEORY

Our contextual anomie/strain theory builds on Robert Merton's anomie theory, Merton's strain theory, Steven Messner and Richard Rosenfeld's institutional anomie theory, as well as Richard Cloward and Lloyd Ohlin's theory of differential opportunity. The theory is a general theory that integrates not only these anomie and strain theories, but also elements of conflict, learning, social control, personality, and opportunity theories.

The scope of the theory is elite deviance (crimes of the powerful). Since anomie and strain theories have historically been used to explain "serious" street crimes,[3] one main contribution of our theory is its application to elite deviance, which we have shown to be far more dangerous and common than street crime.

Our explicit focus is corporate crime. Marshall Clinard and Richard Quinney define corporate crime as "offenses committed by corporate officials for their corporation and the offenses of the corporation itself."[4] A similar definition states corporate crime consists of "illegal acts potentially punishable by criminal sanctions and committed to advance the interests of the corporate organization"[5] Our theory is meant to explain such acts.

Table 3.1 details the main propositions of our theory. Contextual anomie/strain theory explains why elites use maximization to achieve their goals. Given that contextual anomie/strain theory builds upon Merton's theories of anomie and strain, Messner and Rosenfeld's institutional anomie theory, and Cloward and Ohlin's theory of differential opportunity, contextual anomie/strain theory asserts that maximization is explained by

- Prioritization of the goals associated with the American Dream over the legitimate means to achieve those goals (Merton's anomie theory).

- Frustration produced by goal blockage whereby individuals are unable to achieve the goals associated with the American Dream, regardless of how much they have (Merton's strain theory).
- Prioritization of the economy over other noneconomic institutions in America (Messner and Rosenfeld's institutional anomie theory).
- Greater presence of opportunities for deviance in some situations than in others (Cloward and Ohlin's differential opportunity theory).

Table 3.1. Propositions of Contextual Anomie/Strain Theory

1. Greed promotes crime.
2. Greed is emphasized in American culture.

   a. The American Dream promotes greed by emphasizing the cultural goals of society over the institutionalized means to achieve those goals; this weakens norms of law-abiding behavior.
   b. The American Dream promotes greed by emphasizing cultural goals of society that are not reachable because of their infinite nature; this leads to perceptions of strain for people regardless of their level of monetary success.
   c. In America, the health and welfare of the economy are emphasized over the health and welfare of other institutions such as the family, education, and the polity.

3. The cultural goals of the American Dream are learned in schools and promoted by parents and the polity, acting as surrogates for corporate and capitalistic interests.
4. The primary means of satisfying greed by elites is *maximization*—using illegitimate means (i.e., criminality, deviance) in conjunction with legitimate means (i.e., work). Elites simultaneously engage in innovation and conformity to achieve even greater wealth.
5. Maximization is accepted, expected, and even celebrated in given contexts in American society (e.g., corporations).
6. Maximization is learned and promoted in social contexts (e.g., the corporate subculture).

   a. The corporate subculture encourages and at times mandates elite deviance through maximization.
   b. The corporate subculture provides justifications for elite deviance through maximization.
   c. The corporate subculture teaches workers how to commit elite deviance through maximization.

7. Maximization is contingent upon

   a. Individual personality characteristics.
   b. Social and personal controls.
   c. Degree of reward.
   d. Threat of punishment.
   e. Loyalty.
   f. Ideology of executives.
   g. Opportunity.

In other words, contextual anomie/strain theory makes the same assertions about what motivates criminality as other anomie and strain theories—criminality is produced by pressures exerted on people living in American culture. What contextual anomie adds is an explicit focus upon additional pressures that occur in given contexts in American society, such as in the workplace. Our argument is that there are *contexts* in American society whereby individuals, groups, and subcultures are not only living under the pressures to achieve the American Dream that the rest of us live, but also additional pressures to do so that are unique to the given contexts in which they find themselves—hence the name *contextual anomie/strain theory*.

To reiterate, contextual anomie asserts that while everyone experiences pressures of achieving the goals associated with the American Dream, people who find themselves in some contexts will experience additional pressures. Hence, we are acknowledging that some contexts in American society are more criminogenic than others, consistent with the main arguments of Merton, Messner and Rosenfeld, and Cloward and Ohlin.

Given that our focus is on forms of elite deviance, such as corporate crime, we are most interested in how maximization is practiced in "big business." We assert that people working in big business—the corporation—have additional pressures to achieve wealth that emanate from the subcultures of their workplace. That is, in big business, individuals are exposed to additional pressures to achieve wealth through any means, to "maximize wealth" by whatever means necessary, including greed.

In its simplest sense, one might envision an individual who enters the workplace willing, to some degree, to break the law and engage in other deviant behavior because of pressures exerted by the American Dream. The individual becomes more willing to break the law and engage in other deviant behaviors given the norms entrenched in the corporate structure. In the corporate subculture, workers are pressured by managers, bosses, and coworkers to cheat, commit fraud, engage in false advertising, commit insider trading, and so on, in order to "win the game," "beat the competition," and "keep up with the Joneses" (or the Gateses and Buffets, or the corporate competition).

Much research on corporations and corporate managers has assisted us in the development of our theory. In this chapter, we review that research, utilize it to lay out our theory, and illustrate how it can explain maximization.

THE ROLE OF GREED

Recall from chapter 1 that greed is "a selfish and excessive desire for more of something (as money) than is needed,"[6] or "excessive or rapacious desire, esp. for wealth or possessions."[7] Wade Rowland, author of *Greed, Inc.*, defines greed as "a symptom of self-interest, taken too far; all consuming acquisitiveness."[8]

Greed is central to contextual anomie/strain theory, and it is relevant in at least two ways. The first way that greed is important to contextual anomie/strain theory is that all people are encouraged to be greedy simply by living in America. All of us, to some degree or another, are taught by our parents and friends, as well as educational, religious, and employment institutions to pursue wealth and be consumers first and foremost. We are encouraged by these institutions to seek the goals associated with the American Dream. Given that the goal of monetary achievement is one that can never be accomplished—it continues to move higher and higher as one climbs the ladder of social status and income—eventually greed becomes part of the American Dream. That is, people want more than they need, vastly more in many cases, and always more than they have.

Interestingly, the messages of consumerism are quite literally opposed to the traditional values of the family. As Wade Rowland explains, "community, thrift, piety, self-reliance, charity, modesty, love," and so on have been replaced by the values of "pleasure, external appearance, and achievement through consumption."[9]

Research on consumerism demonstrates that greed is promoted in all institutions in the United States, particularly economic institutions. Economics, according to nineteenth-century economist William Stanley Jevons, is "the mechanics of utility and self-interest." So economics is about satisfying "our wants to the utmost with least effort—to procure the greatest amount of what is desirable at the expense of the least that is undesirable"[10] Economic institutions seek enormous wealth, which, as we show later in the chapter, is captured and controlled by a very small group of elites in the country.

Research on consumerism is often discussed around different trends in society and the world—globalization, McDonaldization, and so forth. *Globalization* is an umbrella term for a complex series of economic, social, technological, cultural, demographic, and political changes seen as increasing interdependence, integration, and interaction between people, nations, and extraterritorial entities. It is characterized by a greater international flow of commodities, money, information, people, culture, and the development of technology, organizations, legal systems, and infrastructures that facilitate this movement.[11]

Viewed positively, globalization is the engine of commerce and progress, bringing an increased standard of living and general prosperity to all countries. Economic prosperity is viewed as the foundations of social and political prosperity. Viewed negatively, globalization is an engine of corporate imperialism, or as a process of extending the reach of the empire of capital. This process hides behind notions of prosperity for all, but really amounts to little more than plundering and profiteering through the exploitation of cheap labor and materials and the destruction of local cultures and ecology.[12]

McDonaldization describes the "process by which the principles of the fast-food restaurant are coming to dominate more and more sectors of American society as well as the rest of the world." It is a process that represents the culmination of numerous practices of twentieth-century America, including bureaucratization, scientific management, and assembly line production.[13] Thus, McDonaldization can be viewed as part of globalization.

In his seminal work, *The McDonaldization of Society*, George Ritzer lays out the four elements of McDonaldization:

1. *Efficiency* is "the optimum method for getting from one point to another" or for achieving some goal.[14] In the fast food industry, efficiency is imperative, as the word "fast" implies.
2. *Calculability* is "an emphasis on the quantitative aspects of products sold . . . and services offered. . . . In McDonaldized systems, quantity has become equivalent to quality; a lot of something, or the quick delivery of it, means it must be good."[15] In the fast food industry, more for your money is better than less for your money.
3. *Predictability* refers to "the assurance that products and services will be the same over time and in all locales."[16] In the fast food industry, the goal is to make one's entire dining experience completely consistent with all previous visits; no matter where you go, the product will be exactly the same.
4. *Control* means that as many aspects of production and consumption are governed by strict rules and an emphasis on one way of doing things. In the fast food industry, control is often achieved through the use of nonhuman technology.[17]

Any institution, system, or network of agencies that stresses efficiency, calculability, predictability, and control can be thought of as McDonaldized. Clearly, corporations are characterized by these elements, thus we may think of corporations as McDonaldized.[18] Further, it should be understood that corporations are the key component of globalization. They are, in essence, the engine that drives the process.

Similar to the trends that make up globalization and McDonaldization, Wade Rowland asserts that three trends are changing our society. One is our degree of selfishness and individualism, which has grown in the past century. Many have argued that this is a result of the increased consumerism affiliated with globalization and McDonaldization.[19] Another is a remorseless intrusiveness of markets into all aspects of society, as noted by anomie theorists such as Steven Messner and Richard Rosenfeld.[20] Finally, an explosion in communication technologies—cell phones, laptop computers, personal data assistants—has eroded our personal time. The result is "the wearing-away of all that is most significant in human life, in the face of unrelenting pressures of a selfish, market-driven society."[21] Trends as those identified above promote greed. Because these trends are present in America, there is plenty of reason to expect Americans to be greedy.

The second way that greed is important to contextual anomie/strain theory relates to how some people are encouraged to be even more greedy as a result of the contexts or situations in which they find themselves. For example, corporations strive to maximize wealth, and as it turns out, this is their only expectation.

A corporation is "an association of individuals, created by law or under authority of law, having a continuous existence independent of the existences of its members, and powers and liabilities distinct from those of its members."[22] In modern America, corporations primarily exist to make and sell products and services; this is subsumed under the goal of profit.

According to Francis Cullen, Gray Cavender, William Maakestad, and Michael Benson: "Corporations are the dominant business form in the world today; they are pervasive and wield tremendous economic power. . . . Their economic power is evidenced by wealth and productivity that sometimes exceeds the gross national product of nations."[23]

The positive view of corporations acknowledges that they are "the centerpiece of a free-market capitalist economy" and "a powerful manifestation of entrepreneurial initiative and creativity. They are a major factor in the generally high standard of living Americans typically enjoy."[24] Further, they "produce the seemingly endless range of products we purchase and consume, and they sponsor many of the forms of entertainment (especially television) we enjoy. They are also sponsors of pioneering research in many fields and a crucial element in national defense . . . [and] important benefactors of a large number of charities, public events, institutions of higher learning, and scientific enterprises."[25]

While corporations were intended to be created and maintained for a limited, specific purpose (e.g., building a bridge over a river in one city), they have morphed over time into very powerful permanent entities. They have been transformed "from a creature of the state or some monopoly interest in society with clearly defined public purpose into an all-purpose legal mechanism for facilitating the carrying-on of business within a market economy, its character no longer subject to any meaningful review."[26]

Research on corporations shows that their goal is unlimited acquisitiveness; thus they have no "social good principle." They are, according to many scholars, "singularly self-interested and unable to feel genuine concern for others in any context."[27] This is not to say they do no good; rather they are "adiphoristic—indifferent to right and wrong, good and bad, except insofar as these can be expressed in terms of the corporate equivalents of pleasure and pain—which are profit and loss."[28] The corporation is founded on *moral relativism*, where circumstances rather than principles determine right and wrong.[29]

The paradox is "given that good and bad and right and wrong have real existence and are not just semantic distinctions, and that humans are endowed with a moral drive or impulse that not only enables us to distinguish between these oppositions but impels us toward the good, we nevertheless consent to be governed in our daily lives by institutions that reflect the view that morality is relative and that humans are innately self-serving. Despite the certain knowledge of our moral essence, we acquiesce to an ideology of the market and the corporation that denies it.[30]

Corporations are designed to be greedy. "They are simply not expected to be responsible for social welfare because it is assumed that if they maintain their focus on profit, social good will flow automatically, via the automated processes of the market."[31] Amazingly, when early American corporate executives sought to serve interests other than profit, even courts rejected this idea.

For example, in the case of *Dodge v. Ford* (1916), two brothers took Henry Ford to court to challenge Ford's plans to reduce the price of his Model T automobile for the sake of consumers, but at the expense of corporate profit. The judge agreed with the brothers, "reinstated the dividend and rebuked Ford—who had said in open court that 'business is a service, not a bonanza' and that corporations should run only 'incidentally to make money'—for forgetting that 'a business corporation is organized and carried on primarily for the profit of stockholders'; it could not be run 'for the merely incidental benefit of shareholders and for the primary purpose of benefiting others.'"[32]

Well-known economists, including Milton Friedman and Theodore Leavitt, argued that the fundamental duty of the corporation is to earn profits. These are the words of Friedman: "I call [social responsibility] a fundamentally subversive doctrine in a free society, and say that there is one and only one social responsibility of business to use its resources and engage in activities designed to increase its profits."[33] And Leavitt asserted that "welfare and society are not the corporation's business. Its business is making money. . . . Government's job is not business, and business's job is not government. And unless these functions are resolutely separated in all respects, they are eventually combined in every respect. . . . Altruism, self-denial, charity . . . are vital in certain walks of our life. . . . But for the most part those virtues are alien to competitive economics."[34]

In fact, under the "best interests of the corporation" principle, corporate social responsibility is illegal.[35] The duty of corporate managers is simply to make money; any compromise with this duty is dereliction of duty.[36] This is perhaps the best evidence that when corporations make claims about social responsibility, they do not really mean it.

Wade Rowland goes further, saying that even when codes of ethics state "do the right thing" it means something different to corporations.[37] As noted by Rowland, although truth and contrition are "sometimes simulated in the guise of public-relations devices . . . it is the *appearance* of virtue, rather than virtue itself, that interests corporations. . . . Having a good reputation — having the appearance of virtue — is always a benefit and always, by definition, widely known, while *being* virtuous may not be known to others at all, and it may not be particularly advantageous."[38]

Examples are the ads by "big tobacco" where one major company urges parents to "talk to your kids about *not* smoking." Are we to believe that cigarette companies really want children to *not* start smoking? Given the following facts, this is simply impossible to believe: (1) tobacco companies, like all corporations, are in the business of making money; (2) every dollar spent on advertising is aimed at generating brand loyalty as well as new customers; (3) children and young teenagers are highly influenced by tobacco ads and easily recognize the leading brands; (4) virtually everyone starts smoking before the age of eighteen years, meaning the vast majority of their cash-paying customers started as juveniles; (5) one out of every two smokers will die from smoking-related conditions.[39] If almost no one starts smoking as an adult, who will replace the customers lost to deaths associated with tobacco companies' products? Surely tobacco companies know that without youth smokers, their companies simply cannot maintain profitability in the United States.

Lost in the advertising claims affiliated with this supposed "antismoking" campaign is that tobacco companies have gotten this issue of smoking back on television. It is currently illegal for cigarette companies to advertise their products on television. Yet, this "talk to your kids about not smoking" campaign offers a major tobacco company the opportunity to get cigarettes (and its own logo and company name) back on television. After discussing but a handful of deviant acts by a large tobacco company, Wade Rowland asserts that "the kind of people who run tobacco companies do not appear to resemble any of the people most of us know, unless we happen to work in a clinic for the treatment of mental pathologies. . . . The corporate managers seem to be devoid of the moral sensitivity that is a hallmark of a healthy person."[40]

But what about the individual? What is to be made of the individual people who work for corporations? Don't they have their own morals that conflict with the goal of corporations to seek profit at any cost?

Cullen, Cavender, Maakestad, and Benson, authors of *Corporate Crime Under Attack*, claim: "The most distinctive feature of corporate crime is that it is organizational, not individualistic. This is not to suggest that corporate acts are not the product of individuals; after all, a corporation cannot do anything but through the acts of its agents. . . . The individuals involved in corporate criminality are acting on behalf of the organization and not primarily for direct personal gain—although higher corporate profits, including those obtained illegally, may bring executives such personal benefits as promotions, bonuses, and salary increases."[41]

Additionally, when deviant and criminal policies are enacted within corporations, this "requires the coordination of diverse elements within a corporation. Thus, few violations of the law could be committed without the involvement . . . of many persons within the corporate structure."[42] Corporate crime is organizational in nature rather than individualistic: "[m]assive fraud requires widespread cooperation."[43]

Social science research suggests that individual morals and values are muted in the context of the corporation. Robert Jackall, author of *Moral Mazes: The World of Corporate Managers*, writes that "independent morally evaluative judgments get subordinated to the social intricacies of the bureaucratic workplace. Notions of morality that one might hold and indeed practice outside the workplace—say, some variant of Judeo-Christian ethics—become irrelevant, as do less specifically religious points of principle, unless they mesh with organizational ideologies."[44]

Wade Rowland agrees, stipulating that the "corporate structure, with its rigidly defined goals and its state-sanctioned and reinforced power to discipline, constrains managers to act in ways that most would find ethically abhorrent in their private lives. That is, it forces (or seduces) them to consistently act to enhance corporate profit even at the expense of human welfare."[45] Corporate employees are expected to put aside their own morals and values and take on those of the corporation. The corporation is thus a setting for the work of what Rowland refers to as cyborgs.[46] Rowland's argument is that corporate employees function more like intelligent robots without consideration of individual morality than individual human beings with their own morals.

In this setting, there is little to no tolerance for individual mores.[47] Corporate employees "are under contract, written or implied, to further the aims of the corporation. And even in its broadest construction, the idea that morality involves some concept of human interests, while the moral ethos within which the corporation operates is restricted to contractual obligations and rewards. To ask corporate employees to behave in accordance with authentic moral values, as opposed to the synthetic ethical standards of the corporate machine, is to ask them to invite dismissal and replacement. In the perfectly efficient corporation, there is no room for moral qualms, unless they happen to coincide with corporate aims."[48]

Research shows that "internal factors take precedence over external moral values of expectations in guiding [employees'] actions on the job."[49] This means that the corporate aims of producing and maximizing profit subjugates all other concerns, including right and wrong. There is even evidence that over time, actors within the corporation lose their individuality. They become cut off from their own feelings, values, and morals and instead act almost automatically out of loyalty.[50]

In the corporation, loyalty is expected, and maximization is learned, or passed down from person to person.[51] Edwin Sutherland's theory of differential association posits that individuals learn norms, values, and expectations of behavior from those with whom they associate.[52] The principles of maximization are learned as individuals are socialized into the paramount directive of the American Dream. Within corporations, individuals come to see the mechanism of maximization as the proven method to climb the corporate ladder.

In the corporation, managers "make decisions and give orders in the name of the corporation and not in keeping with their personal standards and values" and employees follow those orders in the name of the corporation even when they conflict with their own personal standards and values.[53] Over time, a corporate subculture emerges and corporate deviance arises in this subculture that consists of "norms and sentiments that make deviance permissible. That is, deviant acts are filtered through a sanitizing, ideological prism, which gives them the appearance of not being criminal or deviant."[54]

Eventually, the values of the corporation become the values of the manager and the employee: "The idea is to capture the hearts and minds of employees—their very identity as persons—and then to define their goals and purposes, managing what they think and feel and not just how they behave on the job."[55] In order for corporations to capture the hearts and minds of employees, employees must check their values at the office door.

Once corporate morality takes over, individuals working in corporations are highly likely to engage in deviant and criminal behavior to satisfy the expectations of the corporation. Rowland states: "In their pursuit of profit, corporations . . . tend to push their behavior to the extreme limits that define the border between what is merely socially unacceptable or unethical and what is illegal. Most humans, even those with a clouded ethical sensibility, will curb themselves long before that borderline is reached, if only because

human society prescribes painful reprisals for ethical misdeeds." Corporations, however, are incapable of curbing their behaviors.[56]

Robert Jackall agrees, saying that "what is right in the corporation is not
what is right in a man's home, or in his church. What is right in the corporation is what the guy above you wants from you. That's what morality is in the
corporation."[57] Win Swenson, who was general counsel at the U.S. Sentencing Commission during the 1990s and who helped write the federal sentencing guidelines for corporations, also concurs. He writes: "Corporate cultures
do create an environment in which individuals engage in misconduct. People
with generally good ethics can go to work for a company where there is a
tremendous amount of pressure to cut corners. And they will cut corners."[58]
This is another way of saying that anomie—norm conflict—is prevalent in
the corporation, that anomie promotes criminality.

Ironically, corporations are now legally treated as individual persons.
The following definition of a corporation illustrates this: "a body formed
and authorized by law to act as a single person although constituted by one
or more persons and legally endowed with various rights and duties including the capacity of succession."[59] In 1886, the U.S. Supreme Court granted
a railroad corporation the status of personhood in the case of *Santa Clara
County v. Southern Pacific Railroad Co.* In so doing, the Court held that it
was effectively "impossible for state governments to regulate railroad tariffs
on the movement of agricultural and other products."[60] Today, as persons,
corporations have "the same rights as human individuals to charge what
they like for their services." Further, a series of Court decisions "granted
corporations the same protections as humans under the First, Fourth, Fifth,
Sixth, and Seventh Amendments" to the U.S. Constitution, covering such
issues as "rights to free speech; freedom from unreasonable searches, and
searches without warrants; freedom from double jeopardy; and trial by jury
in both criminal and civil cases."[61]

Meanwhile, employees are not typically referred to as "employees" or
"workers" by corporate executives but instead as "human resources," who
like land, capital, and products are reduced to measurable outcomes.[62] Not
seeing employees as individual people but rather as resources helps explain
efforts such as downsizing and outsourcing in neoliberalistic economies
aimed at maximizing profit.[63]

In summary, the main problem with corporations "is that they were designed
to duplicate only one aspect of the multifaceted human psyche—greed. They
seek only profit. They reflect none of the redeeming human qualities that
are products of the moral impulse. As the dominant actor in our preeminent
societal institution—the market—the corporation embodies and amplifies the

venal side of human nature, and it does it so successfully that it has reshaped the broad outlines of Western society in its one-dimensional image."[64]

Works such as Joel Bakan's *The Corporation: The Pathological Pursuit of Profit and Power*,[65] David Korten's *When Corporations Rule the World*,[66] Ted Nace's *Gangs of America: The Rise of Corporate Power and the Disabling of Democracy*,[67] and Thom Hartmann's *Unequal Protection: The Rise of Corporate Dominance and the Theft of Human Rights*[68] verify this reality. The corporation is a powerful and pathological organization concerned first and foremost with profit, above everything else, including social good. As such, it is a safe conclusion that corporations are greedy. Further, people who work for corporations find themselves working in a context that promotes greed beyond that produced by exposure to the American Dream.

CONTINGENCIES

Contextual anomie/strain theory, meant to explain various forms of elite deviance, suggests that elites commit deviant acts through maximization in part because of greed. Greed is learned by living in American society as well as in the context of work.

After reviewing cases of offenses by corporations and elites against consumers and the environment; and cases related to unsafe products; securities fraud; fraud by banks, insurance companies, and pension fund industries; government crimes; corruption; medical crime; and computer crime, Stephen Rosoff, Henry Pontell, and Robert Tillman suggest the reader of their book, *Profit Without Honor*, may come to believe that "people are basically greedy and dishonest and, given half a chance, will steal anything they can. Such an interpretation, however, would be far from accurate. Most people, most of the time, do *not* engage in fraud, embezzlement, bribery, and cover-ups. Rather, these acts involve persons occupying certain societal roles and transpire only under certain conditions."[69]

We concur. It is important to understand that our theory attributes maximization to pressures associated with the American Dream, as well as those additional pressures emanating from within corporations. Thus, we are not suggesting that elite deviance and criminality can be explained by simple greed within individual persons working in corporate environments. Instead, it is anomie produced by institutions in American society, exacerbated within the corporation, that promotes greedy criminality. Further, it is strain caused by an inability to achieve the American Dream that promotes greedy criminality. Our theory also posits several contingencies. We use the word "contingencies" to suggest that the likelihood of maximization depends (or is contingent upon) other factors.

Individual Personality Characteristics

First, behaviors inherent to maximization are more likely in certain kinds of people. Criminologists have long asserted causes of criminality that arise from individuals. One of the long-known correlates of criminality is *impulsivity*, or "behaving without giving it much thought, without considering potential future consequences, as if one is motivated only by concerns of pleasure and reward."[70]

Most tests of personality traits in criminal populations have been conducted on street criminals rather than corporate and white-collar offenders. This is likely due to the leading assumption about corporate offenders, that they "are not significantly different, in terms of their personality or psychological make-up, than other people. . . . Indeed, one of the striking things about white-collar offenders is how similar they are to 'respectable' members of society."[71] However, some evidence does show that white-collar and corporate offenders are more likely to be reckless, risk-taking, ambitious, egocentric, and hungry for power.[72]

That corporate offenders are so similar to "respectable" or "law-abiding" members of society lends more credence to our belief that crime is normal in society, even among elites. It also is consistent with one of the main assertions of this chapter—that crime in the context of the corporation is deeply embedded in the structure of the corporations themselves.

One study conducted by Gerhard Blickle and colleagues concluded that "business white-collar crime is predicted by gender (males higher than females), low behavioral self-control, high hedonism, high narcissism, and high conscientiousness."[73] Conscientiousness includes "attributes like striving for competence, order, fulfillment of duties, achievement, self-discipline, and deliberate action."[74] Low behavioral self-control consists of impulsivity as well as other behavioral characteristics.[75]

It is likely that most of the personality traits linked to some forms of corporate malfeasance (e.g., ambitiousness, egocentrism, hunger for power) may also explain legitimate business practice.[76] Still, there is some evidence that business students, many of whom will later go on to become corporate employees, have lower levels of morality and engage in various forms of academic dishonesty (e.g., cheating on tests) than students in other academic disciplines.[77]

Generally speaking, we expect maximization to be more common when corporate executives have personality traits—low behavioral self-control, high hedonism, high narcissism, ambitiousness, egocentrism, hunger for power—that promote deviance. However, this assertion would amount to a tautology since "personality" is commonly defined as a set of behaviors.[78] Further, we believe that maximization will inevitably occur in corporations regardless of the people who work there because the American culture and corporate subculture promote greed and criminality regardless of who is working in the corporation.

Social Controls

Second, social and personal controls are relevant for the likelihood of maximization. Social controls important for corporate crime include the likelihood of punishment that results from criminal and deviant acts, as well as the seriousness of government to regulate business to protect consumers. Clearly, enforcement of laws and regulations that govern corporate behavior is quite weak, especially in comparison to those in place to deal with street crime. According to corporate crime expert David Friedrichs, "corporations are more likely to take certain types of risks if they have reason to believe they can get away with it."[79] It has "not been a principal concern of law enforcement agencies because . . . police have lacked jurisdiction, expertise, and/or resources."[80] This is problematic because *certainty of punishment* is the most important element to deter would-be criminality.[81]

Matthew Robinson, in *Justice Blind?*, demonstrates that less than 5 percent of all law enforcement officers in the United States are focused on acts of elite deviance.[82] After the terrorist attacks of September 11, 2001, the FBI shifted its attention from acts of elite deviance such as white-collar crime to terrorism. In 2006, only 41 percent of FBI agents were assigned to criminal investigations, versus 55 percent who were assigned to counterterrorism or counterintelligence. An examination by Paul Shukovsky, Tracy Johnson, and Daniel Lathrop (2007) found that "thousands of white-collar criminals across the country are no longer being prosecuted in federal court—and, in many cases, not at all—leaving a trail of frustrated victims and potentially billions of dollars in fraud and theft losses. . . . The White House and the Justice Department have failed to replace at least 2,400 agents transferred to counterterrorism squads, leaving far fewer agents on the trail of identity thieves, con artists, hatemongers and other criminals."[83] Outcomes of the shift away from white-collar crime to counterterrorism include the following:

- The number of criminal cases investigated by the FBI nationally has steadily declined. In 2005, the FBI brought more than twenty thousand cases to federal prosecutors, compared with about thirty-one thousand in 2000, a 34 percent decline.

- White-collar crime investigations by the FBI have plummeted in recent years. In 2005, the FBI sent prosecutors thirty-five hundred cases, far less than the more than ten thousand cases assigned to agents in 2000.
- Civil rights investigations (e.g., hate crimes and police abuse) have steadily declined since the late 1990s. FBI agents pursued 65 percent fewer cases in 2005 than they did in 2000.

According to former FBI Executive Assistant Director Dale Watson (who oversaw counterterrorism operations): "The budget should be backfilled with additional agents. We've got to do this. But you could request 2,000 agents for white collar, and it would never see the light of day. . . . We realized we were going to have to pull out of some areas—bank fraud, investment fraud, ID theft—cases that protect the financial infrastructure of the country." In fact, the number of white-collar crime cases investigated and referred for prosecution declined 68 percent between 1997 and 2005, bank fraud cases declined 69 percent, and civil rights cases declined 71 percent. Virtually all of these declines occurred after 2001. During the same time period, the number of child pornography cases increased 213 percent, domestic terrorism cases increased 90 percent, and international terrorism cases increased 64 percent.

Given the federal cutback in white-collar investigations, states would be left to pick up the slack; however, budget cuts have made this impossible. The net effect of this change is that not only are white-collar offenders less likely to be arrested and prosecuted, they are also likely to spend less time in jail or prison than before. The main reason is that when convicted in state court, white-collar offenders generally receive much lighter sentences than if convicted and sentenced in federal courts.[84]

President Bush's Corporate Fraud Task Force—created after a wave of corporate crime in the early twenty-first century—consists of the deputy attorney general, two assistant attorneys general, the director of the Federal Bureau of Investigation, and seven U.S. attorneys.[85] Jeffrey Reiman and Paul Leighton's (2003) analysis of the task force suggests that it amounts to "huff and puff and . . . do little."[86]

Prosecutions by the task force have been few and far between. An editorial in the *Multinational Monitor* asks: "Does corporate crime pay? Increasingly, not only does it pay, it's not even prosecuted—even when the corporate crime cops have the goods on the bad guys."[87] The reason is because rather than prosecuting corporate offenders, prosecutors are entering into two kinds of agreements with them. One is a nonprosecution agreement where the prosecutor agrees to not even charge the corporation "in exchange for fines, cooperation and changes in corporate structure." Another is a deferred prosecution agreement, where changes are filed but dropped "if the company abides by promises to the prosecutor."[88]

Given these trends, we expect maximization to be widely prevalent in the corporate world. Conversely, serious efforts to hold corporations accountable for their culpable, harmful acts ought to reduce maximization.

As for the regulation of business, those agencies responsible for regulating corporations "are greatly understaffed and underfunded."[89] The reason? U.S. government agencies are probusiness and the dominant business ideology says that government regulation is nothing more than "meddling."[90] Proponents of a free market economy contend that regulation of business is not needed because "unrestrained competition lowers prices and impels producers to improve the quality and safety of their goods and services."[91] In other words, protection of consumers requires consumers buying the right goods in order to protect themselves, consistent with the notion of *caveat emptor* (let the buyer beware). Further, corporations hold that most are law-abiding, which means that regulation really isn't necessary. This contradicts the evidence about corporate crime that we demonstrate in chapters 4 and 5.

An example of weak regulation is that by the Environmental Protection Agency (EPA). It utilizes a self-policing policy "to persuade companies to improve their environmental performance by disclosing and correcting environmental violations in exchange for the elimination or reduction of gravity-based penalties and the promise not to initiate a civil or criminal investigation of the violation. It is market-based in that it increases regulatory efficiency and improves environmental performance when compared to forms of traditional enforcement because environmental violations are detected and corrected more quickly."[92]

Another example is evident at the Consumer Product Safety Commission (CPSC), which is an independent federal regulatory agency that conducts research on products to determine which are hazardous. The CPSC develops voluntary standards with industry, issues and enforces mandatory standards for product safety, bans consumer products that are proven unsafe, and informs consumers of product safety recalls and issues. It was created by Congress in 1972 to protect the public "against unreasonable risks of injuries associated with consumer products."

The CPSC has more than three hundred voluntary standards to be followed by business, plus about fifty mandatory regulations, and has a "Disclosure Rule," which requires that product manufacturers report defective products as soon as they are discovered if they pose threats to consumers. However, most of their standards are voluntary and corporations are essentially allowed to police themselves.

A recent example dealing with the CPSC illustrates the poor nature of regulation of business in the United States. In 2005, government scientists tested sixty soft, vinyl lunchboxes and found that one in five contained "amounts of lead that medical experts consider unsafe—and several had more than 10 times hazardous levels."[93] However, the CPSC did not tell the public! Instead, it released a statement saying they found "no instances of hazardous levels." Further, the CPSC did not release its actual test results, citing regulations that are meant to protect manufacturers from making such information public. Only after the Associated Press issued a Freedom of Information Act request did the CPSC send along documents that led to the discovery of the test results: "The results of the first type of test, looking for the actual lead content of the vinyl, showed that 20 percent of the bags had more than 600 parts per million of lead—the federal safe level for paint and other products. The highest level was 9,600 ppm, more than 16 times the federal standard. But the CPSC did not use those results."[94]

Amazingly, a CPSC spokesperson said: "When it comes to a lunchbox, it's carried. The food that you put in the lunchbox may have an outer wrapping, a baggie, so there isn't direct exposure. The direct exposure would be if kids were putting their lunchboxes in their mouth, which isn't a common way for children to interact with their lunchbox."[95]

Alexa Engelman, a researcher at the Oakland, California–based Center for Environmental Health, reacted: "They found levels that we consider very high. . . . They knew this all along and they didn't take action on it. It's upsetting to me. Why are we, as a country, protecting the companies? We should be protecting the kids. I don't think in this instance they did their job."[96]

Since the Food and Drug Administration (FDA) reviewed the test results and sent a letter to lunchbox manufacturers telling them that the lunchboxes may be dangerous, it appears the action of the CPSC was negligent in nature. Further, Wal-Mart stopped selling such lunchboxes due to safety concerns.

High levels of lead in blood can lead to learning problems, reduced intelligence, hyperactivity, and attention deficit disorder. No level of lead in the blood is considered safe.[97] This compelled Dr. Bruce Lamphear, a lead poisoning specialist at the Children's Hospital Medical Center in Cincinnati, Ohio, to say: "I don't think the Consumer Product Safety Commission has lived up to its role to protect kids from lead. . . . As a public agency, their work should be transparent. And if one is to err on the side of protecting children rather than protecting lunch box makers, then certainly you would want to lower the levels."[98]

The CPSC does not test products, nor recommend products, nor investigate any claims with regard to automobiles and vehicles, tires, boats, alcohol, tobacco, firearms, food, drugs, cosmetics, pesticides, or medical devices (these are the domain of other regulatory agencies, including the National Highway Traffic Safety Administration or NHTSA, the U.S. Coast Guard, the Food and Drug Administration or FDA, and the Bureau of Alcohol, Tobacco, and Firearms or ATF). The CPSC also does not investigate false advertising, fraud, or poor product quality unrelated to safety (this is the domain of the Federal Trade Commission or FTC) or claims dealing with work-related incidents (this is the domain of the Occupational Safety and Health Administration or OSHA).

Deregulation of business has been a major priority since the Ronald Reagan presidency. Deregulation occurs when a government passes laws to limit its own control over an industry. In the 1980s, budgets of OSHA, the CPSC, and FTC were slashed, and requirements relating to pharmaceutical and automotive safety were lifted or softened.[99] Most of these changes in policy were attached as "riders" to large bills in Congress. Deregulation clearly played a significant role in the savings and loans scandals of the 1980s and early 1990s, which we will discuss in chapter 4. When deregulation is the norm, we expect maximization to be widely prevalent in the corporate world. Conversely, serious efforts to regulate corporations for public safety ought to reduce maximization.

The history of government regulation has been one of businesses regulating themselves for their own benefit and gain. Many regulators are former corporate executives or go to work for corporations after their regulating days are over.[100] Thus, there is a double standard of justice in the United States. While we spend tens of billions of dollars each year fighting street crimes that produce relatively minor harms, we allow businesses to police themselves, and we make "little effort to enforce the law against [white-collar and corporate] criminals. When we do catch them at their nefarious deeds, we tap them on the wrist, make them say they are sorry, and send them about their criminal business."[101]

The National Highway Traffic Safety Administration (NHTSA) is part of the U.S. Department of Transportation and was created in 1970. It is the agency charged with reducing deaths, injuries, and economic losses resulting from motor vehicle crashes. NHTSA sets and enforces safety performance standards for motor vehicles and automobile equipment, and it investigates safety defects in motor vehicles. This agency also provides consumer information on motor vehicle safety topics, grants funds for state and local governments to assist them with conducting local highway safety programs, sets and enforces fuel economy standards, promotes automotive safety through the use of safety belts, child safety seats, and airbags, and conducts research on driver behavior and traffic to suggest safety improvements.

The Food and Drug Administration (FDA) was created under a different name in the early 1900s and became known as the FDA in 1930. Its main responsibilities include ensuring the safety of our food, cosmetics, medicine and medical devices, and some products such as microwave ovens. It also oversees feed and drugs for pets and farm animals. The FDA employs more than nine thousand employees who are responsible for visiting more than sixteen thousand facilities annually.

Like NHTSA, the FDA operates mainly by voluntary recalls, but it also can, by court order, force defective products from the market. The specific products it regulates include biologics (such as blood supply), cosmetics, radiation-emitting products (such as microwaves), and food products (except for meat and poultry, which are regulated by the Food and Safety Inspection Service of the U.S. Department of Agriculture).

Regulatory agencies in the United States are understaffed and have great difficulty regulating the products within their jurisdictions. Essentially, regulatory agencies such as the FDA operate under the assumption of *caveat emptor*, or let the buyer beware. The burden rests on the consumer to avoid being injured or killed by defective products. Amazingly, there is only one person in the entire country charged with inspecting children's toys—in spite of the recent spate of recalls of toys due to dangerous levels of lead paint—and his name is Bob!

Congress has passed legislation aimed at strengthening reporting requirements of corporations to regulatory agencies. However, since there is no corporate police force, the American people are counting on the corporations to be honest in policing themselves. Joel Bakan points out the hypocrisy of letting potential corporate criminals regulate themselves: "No one would seriously suggest that individuals should regulate themselves, that laws against murder, assault, and theft are unnecessary because people are socially responsible. Yet oddly, we are asked to believe that corporate persons—institutional psychopaths who lack any sense of moral conviction and who have the power and motivation to cause harm and devastation in the world—should be left free to govern themselves."[102]

This is dangerous because corporations view abiding by the law as a matter of simple costs and benefits.[103] Corporate managers follow a "secular, pragmatic, utilitarian calculus" to carry out costs–benefits analyses and utilize "a vast array of vocabularies of motives and accounts to explain, or excuse and justify, expedient action."[104]

Such vocabulary is utilized to justify culpable harms by corporations—for example, "in the textile industry, cotton dust becomes an 'air-borne particulate' and byssinosis or brown lung becomes a 'symptom complex.' In the chemical industry, spewing highly toxic hydrogen fluoride into a neighboring community's air is characterized as a 'release beyond the fence line.'"[105] The tobacco industry uses "sidestream smoke" in place of "secondhand smoke." Shockingly, even regulatory agencies do this. For example, the Department of Agriculture referred to the powdered bone in reprocessed meats as "calcium"; the Environmental Protection Agency called acid rain "poorly buffered precipitation"; the National Transportation Safety Board in the Federal Aviation Agency Accident Investigation Records calls airplane crashes "controlled flights into terrain."[106]

Research shows that corporations use *techniques of neutralization* to justify their harmful acts.[107] Corporate executives deny responsibility for their acts, and also deny that their victims are harmed in any way. They also appeal to higher loyalties when acting in a deviant manner and condemn those who condemn them for their acts.[108] Serious regulation of business reduces not only opportunities for deviance but also the presentation of neutralization techniques to justify the harmful acts of corporations.

Personal Controls

Third, as for personal controls, *low self-control* is popular in the criminological literature as an explanation for many forms of crime. Low self-control consists of impulsivity, risk-seeking behaviors, a self-centered orientation, a volatile temper, and a preference for simple and physical activities.[109] However, low self-control may not be well-suited for explaining corporate crime. For example, it is understood that corporate executives are not impulsive, although they take certain risks (even with other people's money) and may act in their own self-interests.

Instead, *control surpluses* may play a role. Control balance theory predicts that those with control surpluses and control deficits are most prone to deviant behavior. Control surpluses suggest some people have greater control over others than others have over them, and control deficits indicate that some people experience more control exerted over them than they exert over others.[110]

Charles Tittle, founder of control balance theory, posited that control surpluses relate to acts of exploitation, plunder, and decadence by the wealthy and by corporations. Examples of these harmful acts include price-fixing, massive pollution, and repression of employees, respectively.[111] One example of corporate deviance provided by Tittle is the authorized "dumping of toxic waste into rivers after having carefully calculated that those who would be harmed most immediately—farmers and fishers along the river—will not be able to do much about it." He continues: "Business people do these things when they become aware that they, through the corporate vehicle, enjoy a surplus of control, which can be extended by this means. Of course, in the case of corporate executives, such provocations are probably quite common, since concern with business operations and profits is a continuous, routine activity (which is why exploitation is so common)."[112]

A test of control balance theory by Nicole Piquero and Alex Piquero found that "control surpluses rather than control deficits relate to exploitative acts in the corporate context."[113] This is logical given the amount of power—control—executives in corporations exercise over others and how little is exercised over them by the law and regulatory agencies.

Nicole Piquero, M. Lyn Exum, and Sally Simpson (2005) add the concept of "desire-for-control" as a potential explanation of corporate crime. *Desire-for-control* generally refers to "the general wish to be in control over everyday life events."[114] Persons who have a high desire-for-control are assertive, decisive, active, influential, manipulative, and tend to be leaders. Piquero and colleagues speculate that managers with a high desire-for-control "may come to believe that they have to do something—even if it is criminal—in order to survive, get by and perhaps more importantly, get ahead."[115] Their study suggests that individuals who desire a high degree of control may be more likely to violate the law when they cannot achieve their goals legally, as predicted by strain theory. Maximization is thus more likely when corporate executives sense they are unable to achieve their goals through conformity alone, thereby requiring innovation.

Reward and Punishment

Fourth, degree of reward affects the likelihood of maximization. As explained by anomie and strain theories, striving for success is a moral imperative in the United States.[116] We hold this to be a significant source of both legal (i.e., conformity) and illegal behavior (i.e., innovation) in society. We expect that when potential reward is higher, the likelihood of maximization is higher.

Similarly, the threat of punishment affects the likelihood of maximization. Although many believe corporations act rationally and thus corporate behaviors can be explained by rational choices approaches,[117] it is a safe conclusion to say that corporations are not much concerned with harms caused by their actions, at least when enforcement and regulation are weak. Harms are instead referred to as "externalities" by corporations—outcomes that are made "external to the corporation's interests and concern and are instead turned over to the wider public to deal with." Examples include pollution associated with the manufacture of products, social disorganization caused by downsizing and outsourcing, violent behavior produced by exposure to media, and so on. As noted by Wade Rowland: "Externalities are a way of privatizing profit while socializing costs."[118]

According to Joel Bakan, corporations are designed to externalize their costs. They are "deliberately programmed, indeed legally compelled, to externalize costs without regard for the harm it may cause to people, communities, and the natural environment. Every cost it can unload onto someone else is a benefit to itself, a direct route to profit."[119] This suggests that potential costs are minimized by corporations when they are outweighed by potential profits.

We predict that individuals working for corporations are less likely to engage in criminality and deviance on behalf of the corporation when there is a significant threat of punishment. Unfortunately, there is currently little risk of punishment for committing criminal and deviant acts in corporations and much risk of sanctions for *not* committing criminal and deviant acts when it is expected and/or required as part of one's job.

Loyalty

Fifth, loyalty is clearly important, as well: "Corporate employees, as condition of employment, place responsibility to the corporation ahead of everything else, including responsibility to humanity."[120] Sociologists and psychologists have studied corporate decision making and have found that corporate employees act as agents of the corporation following *routinized scripts* even in risky situations rather than as individual people motivated by morality.

David Simon and Frank Hagan assert: "Decisions to commit deviant acts—even murder—are carried out within established routines."[121] That is, corporate deviance does not typically require thought by individual employees. It is normal, expected, and routinized in the large, complex nature of modern organizations. Simon and Hagan explain that "specialized tasks involve the same routines, whether they are deviant or legitimate."[122] The Ford Pinto case, discussed in chapter 5, is an excellent example of how corporate employees follow scripts that allow dangerous products to reach the marketplace in spite of the dangers they pose.[123]

According to David Simon, "the authority of elites . . . is obeyed in large measure because it is recognized as legitimate."[124] That is, corporate crime is likely "where the law is unclear or when common organizational practices discredit the significance of the violation (i.e., it is common business practice)."[125] Ultimately, individuals working for major corporations end up committing deviant and criminal behaviors, while simultaneously failing to see them as wrong or illegal. Wade Rowland agrees, suggesting that the nature of corporate crime is committed by people seeking profit "who believe themselves to be operating in good faith within an ethical framework that is widely recognized and respected."[126] This is another way of acknowledging that crime is normal in the context of the corporation.

The reason loyalty is so important in maximization is simple: loyalty means moving up in the corporate organization; disloyalty means failing.[127] As noted by Robert Jackall: "Top management always exerts pressure on subordinates, and subordinates on themselves, to do what they believe has to be done. There are few more effective legitimating rationales in the corporate world than the invocation of [a corporate manager's] authoritatively approved 'goals,' 'objectives,' or 'mission.'"[128]

Nicole Piquero and Alex Piquero agree, stating that "the motivation for individuals who engage in acts of corporate crime is not personal benefit but instead loyalty to the company. The goal, then, of corporate crime is to advance corporate interests."[129] Similarly, Piquero and colleagues add that "the main premise of corporate crime is not that individuals offend for personal benefit; rather, individuals engage in illegality in order to advance corporate interests."[130]

We expect that maximization will be more common in corporations with a high expectation for loyalty among their employees. Conversely, corporations that allow and encourage their employees to "do the right thing" rather than seek profit at any cost will host less maximization.

Executive Ideology

Sixth, the ideology of the leading executives within corporations also affects the likelihood of maximization. When corporate executives actively promote deviance, deviance is more likely to occur. For example, Stephen Rosoff, Henry Pontell, and Robert Tillman ask: "Why do some organizations promote 'deviance' while others do not? Sometimes it is simply a matter of the greed of the individuals leading the organization."[131]

Maximization is more likely when corporations are led by executives with an ideology that justifies and promotes deviant and illegal behavior. Conversely, maximization is less likely when leading agents of corporations do not justify and promote such behavior, either directly or indirectly, as well as when they actually discourage and sanction bad behaviors. Since greed is so widespread within corporations, there is likely little variation in the ideology of corporate executives with regard to the acceptability of illegal and deviant behaviors to achieve wealth; yet, we can envision scenarios whereby particularly deviant individuals leading corporations may be more organized and committed to such behaviors than in others. In those cases, maximization would be more likely.

Opportunity

Finally, opportunity is obviously very important to understanding any deviant or criminal behavior. Simply stated, without the opportunity for behavior, behavior cannot occur, regardless of the motivation.[132] Maximization is more likely to occur when there are opportunities for it. Conversely, maximization is less likely to occur when there is less opportunity.

A major premise of our argument is that there is tremendous opportunity for maximization within corporations. Therefore, we expect maximization to be widespread. However, with efforts to reduce maximization through means such as increased regulation and punishment of would-be offenders, as well as rewards for law-abiding behaviors, we expect maximization to be reduced.

We now turn to the issue of how our theory can be used to explain corporate crime, In chapter 4, we apply our theory to property crime by corporations, and in chapter 5 we use it to explain violent acts by corporations.

NOTES

1. Messner, Steven, and Richard Rosenfeld (2001). *Crime and the American Dream.* Belmont, CA: Wadsworth, citing economist Freeman, Richard (1988). Why do so many American young men commit crimes and what might we do about it? Working paper 5451. Cambridge, MA: National Bureau of Economic Research.

2. Matza, David (1964). *Delinquency and Drift.* New York: Transaction Publishers.

3. Robinson, Matthew (2004). *Why Crime? An Integrated Systems Theory of Antisocial Behavior.* Upper Saddle River, NJ: Prentice Hall.

4. Clinard, Marshall, and Richard Quinney (1973). *Criminal Behavior Systems: A Typology* (2nd ed.), 188. New York: LexisNexis.

5. Cullen, Francis, Gray Cavender, William Maakestad, and Michael Benson (2006). *Corporate Crime Under Attack* (2nd ed.). Cincinnati, OH: Anderson, 9.

6. Merriam-Webster Online Dictionary. Entry for "greed." Retrieved July 25, 2007, from www.merriam-webster.com/dictionary/greed.

7. Dictionary.com. Entry for "greed." Retrieved July 27, 2007, from dictionary .reference.com/browse/greed.

8. Rowland, Wade (2005). *Greed, Inc.: Why Corporations Rule Our World and How We Let It Happen.* Toronto, Canada: Thomas Allen Publishers, xviii.

9. Rowland, *Greed Inc.*, 159.

10. Quoted in McConnell, Campbell (1981). *Economics* (8th ed.). New York: McGraw Hill.

11. Reck, Greg (2007). Personal communication. November 2007. Boone, NC.

12. Reck, Personal communication.

13. Ritzer, George (2000). *The McDonaldization of Society.* Thousand Oaks, CA: Pine Forge Press, 1.

14. Ritzer, *The McDonaldization of Society*, 12.

15. Ritzer, *The McDonaldization of Society*, 12.

16. Ritzer, *The McDonaldization of Society*, 13.

17. Ritzer, *The McDonaldization of Society*, p. 2000: 236.

18. Ritzer, George (2006). *The McDonaldization Reader.* Thousand Oaks, CA: Pine Forge Press.

19. Alfino, Mark, John Caputo, and Robin Wynyard (1998). *McDonaldization Revisited: Critical Essays on Consumer Culture.* Westport, CT: Praeger.

20. Messner, Steven, and Richard Rosenfeld (1994). *Crime and the American Dream.* New York: Wadsworth.

21. Rowland, *Greed Inc.*, xvii–xviii.

22. Dictionary.com (2008). Entry for "corporation." Retrieved January 5, 2008, from http://dictionary.reference.com/browse/corporation.

23. Cullen et al., *Corporate Crime Under Attack*, 66.

24. Friedrichs, David (1995). *Trusted Criminals: White Collar Crime in Contemporary Society.* Belmont, CA: Wadsworth, 67.

25. Friedrichs, *Trusted Criminals*, 67.

26. Rowland, *Greed Inc.*, 82.

27. Bakan, Joel (2005). *The Corporation: The Pathological Pursuit of Profit and Power.* New York: Free Press, 56.

28. Rowland, *Greed Inc.*, 84.

29. Rowland, *Greed Inc.*, xxi.

30. Rowland, *Greed Inc.*, 74.

31. Rowland, *Greed Inc.*, 93.

32. Rowland, *Greed Inc.*, 94.

33. Friedman, Milton (1970). The social responsibility of business is to increase its profits. *New York Sunday Times,* September 13, 32.

34. Leavitt, Theodore (1979). The dangers of social responsibility. In Thomas Beauchamp and Norma Bowie (eds.), *Ethical Theory and Business.* Chicago: University of Chicago Press, 138.

35. Bakan, Joel (2004). *The Corporation.* Toronto: Viking, 36.

36. Bakan (2005), *The Corporation.*

37. Rowland, *Greed Inc.*, 152.

38. Rowland, *Greed Inc.*, 100.

39. Brandt, Allan (2007). *The Cigarette Century: The Rise, Fall, and Deadly Persistence of the Product That Defined America.* New York: Basic Books; Glantz, Stanton, John Slade, Lisa Bero, Peter Hanauer, and Deborah Barnes (1997). *The Cigarette Papers.* Berkeley, CA: University of California Press; Kluger, Richard (1997). *Ashes to Ashes: America's Hundred-Year Cigarette War, the Public Health,*

and the Unabashed Triumph of Philip Morris. New York: Knopf; Mollenkamp, Carrick, Joseph Menn, and Adam Levy (1998). *The People vs. Big Tobacco: How the States Took on the Cigarette Giants*. New York: Bloomberg; Orey, Michael (1999). *Assuming the Risk: The Mavericks, the Lawyers, and the Whistle-Blowers Who Beat Big Tobacco*. New York: Little, Brown and Company; Zegart, Dan (2001). *Civil Warriors: The Legal Siege on the Tobacco Industry*. Surrey, UK: Delta.

40. Rowland, *Greed Inc.*, 111–12.

41. Cullen et al., *Corporate Crime Under Attack*, 9.

42. Cullen et al., *Corporate Crime Under Attack*, 9.

43. Reiman, Jeffrey (2006). *The Rich Get Richer and the Poor Get Prison* (8th ed.). Boston, MA: Allyn & Bacon, 120.

44. Jackall, Robert (1988). *Moral Mazes: The World of Corporate Managers*. New York: Oxford University Press, 105.

45. Rowland, *Greed Inc.*, 120.

46. Rowland, *Greed Inc.*, 123, 128.

47. Rowland, *Greed Inc.*, 175.

48. Rowland, *Greed Inc.*, 193.

49. Friedrichs, *Trusted Criminals*, 223.

50. Harper, Jan (1988). *Quiet Desperation: The Truth about Successful Men*. New York: Werner Books.

51. Rowland, *Greed Inc.*, 118.

52. Sutherland, Edwin (1947). *Principles of Criminology* (4th ed). Philadelphia, PA: JB Lippincott.

53. Rowland, *Greed Inc.*, 119.

54. Simon, David (2006). *Elite Deviance* (8th ed.). Boston, MA: Allyn & Bacon, 290.

55. Rowland, *Greed Inc.*, 126–27.

56. Rowland, *Greed Inc.*, 98–99.

57. Jackall, *Moral Mazes*, 225.

58. *Multinational Monitor* (2005). Corporate crime and prosecution: An Interview with Win Swenson. November/December.

59. Merriam-Webster Online (2008). Entry for "corporation." Retrieved January 5, 2008, from www.merriam-webster.com/dictionary/corporation.

60. Rowland, *Greed Inc.*, 86–87.

61. Rowland, *Greed Inc.*, 87.

62. Rowland, *Greed Inc.*, 121.

63. Rowland, *Greed Inc.*, 123–24.

64. Rowland, *Greed Inc.*, xxi.

65. Bakan (2005), *The Corporation*.

66. Korten, David (2001). *When Corporations Rule the World*. San Francisco, CA: Berrett-Koehler Publishers.

67. Nace, Ted (2005). *Gangs of America: The Rise of Corporate Power and the Disabling of Democracy*. San Francisco, CA: Berrett-Koehler Publishers.

68. Hartmann, Thom (2004). *Unequal Protection: The Rise of Corporate Dominance and the Theft of Human Rights*. New York: Rodale Books.

69. Rosoff, Stephen, Henry Pontell, and Robert Tillman (2002). *Profit Without Honor: White-Collar Crime and the Looting of America* (2nd ed.). Upper Saddle River, NJ: Prentice Hall, 217.

70. Robinson, Matthew (2004). *Why Crime? An Integrated Systems Theory of Antisocial Behavior.* Upper Saddle River, NJ: Prentice Hall, 103.

71. Rosoff, Pontell, and Tillman, *Profit Without Honor*, 455.

72. Friedrichs, *Trusted Criminals*, 217.

73. Blickle, Gerhard, Alexander Schlegel, Pantaleon Fassbender, and Uwe Klein (2006). Some personality correlates of business white-collar crime. *Applied Psychology: An International Review* 55(2): 221.

74. Blickle et al., Some personality correlates of business white-collar crime, 224.

75. Gottfredson, Michael, and Travis Hirschi (1990). *A General Theory of Crime.* Stanford, CA: Stanford University Press.

76. Piquero, Nicole, Lyn M. Exum, and Sally Simpson (2005). Integrating the desire-for-control and rational choice in a corporate crime context. *Justice Quarterly* 22(2): 262.

77. Rowland, *Greed Inc.*, 113.

78. Robinson, *Why Crime?*

79. Friedrichs, *Trusted Criminals*, 16.

80. Friedrichs, *Trusted Criminals*, 271.

81. Robinson, Matthew (2009). *Justice Blind? Ideals and Realities of American Criminal Justice* (3rd ed.). Upper Saddle River, NJ: Prentice Hall.

82. Robinson, *Justice Blind?*

83. Shukovsky, Paul, Tracy Johnson, and Daniel Lathrop (2007). The FBI's terrorism trade-off. Focus on national security after 9/11 means that the agency has turned its back on thousands of white-collar crimes. *Seattle PI*, April 11. Retrieved April 12, 2007, from seattlepi.nwsource.com/national/311046_fbiterror11.html.

84. Robinson, *Justice Blind?*

85. Cooney, John (2006). Multi-jurisdictional and successive prosecution of environmental crimes: The case for a consistent approach. *The Journal of Criminal Law & Criminology* 96(2): 435.

86. Reiman, J., and P. Leighton (2003). Getting tough on corporate crime? Enron and a year of corporate financial scandals. Retrieved July 1, 2004, from www.stopviolence.com.

87. *Multinational Monitor*, Corporate crime and punishment.

88. *Multinational Monitor*, Corporate crime and punishment.

89. Friedrichs, *Trusted Criminals,* 285.

90. Simon, *Elite Deviance*, 39.

91. Rosoff, Pontell, and Tillman, *Profit Without Honor*, 43.

92. Stretesky, Paul (2006). Corporate self-policing and the environment. *Criminology* 44(3): 672–73.

93. Mendoza, Martha (2007). How gov't decided lunch box lead levels. Associated Press. Retrieved February 18, 2007, from www.washingtonpost.com/wp-dyn/content/article/2007/02/18/AR2007021800528_pf.html.

94. Mendoza, How gov't decided lunch box lead levels.

95. Mendoza, How gov't decided lunch box lead levels.

96. Mendoza, How gov't decided lunch box lead levels.

97. Robinson, *Why Crime?*

98. Mendoza, How gov't decided lunch box lead levels.

99. Kappeler, Victor, Michael Blumberg, and Gary Potter (2000). *The Mythology of Crime and*
Criminal Justice (3rd ed.). Prospect Heights, IL: Waveland Press, 135.

100. Hagan, Frank (1998). *Political Crime, Ideology, and Criminality*. Boston, MA: Allyn and Bacon.

101. Kappeler, Blumberg, and Potter, *The Mythology of Crime and Criminal Justice*, 134.

102. Bakan (2005), *The Corporation*, 110.

103. Bakan (2005), *The Corporation*, 79.

104. Jackall, *Moral Mazes*, 127, 134.

105. Jackall, *Moral Mazes*, 136.

106. Jackall, *Moral Mazes*, 136–37.

107. Sykes, Gresham, and David Matza (1957). Techniques of neutralization. *American Sociological Review* 22: 664–70.

108. Simon, *Elite Deviance*, 291–92.

109. Gottfredson and Hirschi, *A General Theory of Crime*.

110. Tittle, Charles (1995). *Control Balance*. Boulder, CO: Westview.

111. Tittle, Charles (2004). Refining control balance theory. *Theoretical Criminology* 8: 395–428.

112. Tittle, *Control Balance*, 164.

113. Piquero, Nicole, and Alex Piquero (2006). Control balance and exploitative corporate crime. *Criminology* 44(2): 397.

114. Piquero, Exum, and Simpson, Integrating the desire-for-control, 252–80.

115. Piquero, Exum, and Simpson, Integrating the desire-for-control, 260.

116. Jackall, *Moral Mazes*, 43.

117. Braithwaite, John, and Toni Makkai (1991). Testing an expected utility model or corporate deterrence. *Law & Society Review* 25: 7–40; Jamieson, Katherine (1994). *The Organization of Corporate Crime*. Thousand Oaks, CA: Sage; Paternoster, Raymond, and Sally Simpson (1996). Sanction threats and appeals to morality: Testing a rational choice model of corporate crime. *Law & Society Review* 30: 549–83; Simpson, Sally, and Christopher Koeper (1992). Deterring corporate crime. *Criminology* 30: 347–75.

118. Rowland, *Greed Inc.*, 115.

119. Bakan (2005), *The Corporation*, 72–73.

120. Rowland, *Greed Inc.*, 117.

121. Simon, David, and Frank Hagan (1999). *White-Collar Deviance*. Boston, MA: Allyn & Bacon.

122. Simon and Hagan. *White-Collar Deviance*.

123. Rowland, *Greed Inc.*, 118.

124. Simon, *Elite Deviance*, 290.

125. Piquero, Exum, and Simpson, Integrating the desire-for-control, 256.

126. Rowland, *Greed Inc.*, 109.

127. Jackall, *Moral Mazes*, 45.

128. Jackall, *Moral Mazes*, 117.

129. Piquero and Piquero, Control balance and exploitative corporate crime, 404.

130. Piquero, Exum, and Simpson, Integrating the desire-for-control, 256.

131. Rosoff, Pontell, and Tillman, *Profit Without Honor*, 460.

132. Paulsen, Derek, and Matthew Robinson (2004). *Spatial Aspects of Crime: Theory and Practice*. Boston, MA: Allyn & Bacon.

4

Maximization and Elite Property Crime

Corporate crime inflicts far more damage on society than all street crime combined. Whether in bodies or injuries or dollars lost, corporate crime and violence wins by a landslide.

—Russell Mokhiber, "Twenty Things You Should Know about Corporate Crime" (2007)[1]

As we showed in chapter 1, acts of elite deviance—including corporate crime—are far more damaging than street crime. The above statement by corporate crime expert Russell Mokhiber is correct—when it comes to harms caused by street crime and corporate crime, it is not even close.

In this chapter, we apply our theory of elite deviance—*contextual anomie/ strain theory*—to show how the majority of corporate crime involves maximization. Our approach in this chapter is to (1) introduce specific forms of elite deviance, describing them in detail with specific examples; (2) illustrate how these forms of corporate crime involve maximization; and (3) demonstrate how our theory explains these behaviors. In this chapter, our focus is on forms of corporate crimes committed for property gain, including fraud and deceptive advertising. While this chapter does not analyze all forms of corporate crime (in part because there are so many), we are confident that our theory explains most forms of elite deviance.

FORMS OF ELITE DEVIANCE

Fraud

Definition

As we showed in chapter 1, *fraud* is a form of theft whereby a person is deprived of his or her money or property through deceit, trickery, or lies. That is, fraud is theft plus deceit. Fraud is the most common crime in the United States. This is because, while theft requires face-to-face contact with a criminal (or direct contact with a person's property), fraud can be committed any time there is a property transaction. Any time someone buys, sells, or trades something, there is a potential for fraud. Fraud can also occur when a person brings any product in for service (e.g., automotive repair fraud), or when a service person is called to repair a product (e.g., VCR/DVD repair fraud).

Fraud can be perpetrated by individuals through street crime and white-collar crime, but the largest forms of fraud involve large corporations creating huge losses.[2] Our focus in this chapter is on fraud committed by corporations as part of normal business practice.

Examples

There are scores of different types of fraud committed by corporations. After reviewing the latest information available for corporate and white-collar crime, Jeffrey Reiman reports that consumer fraud costs Americans about $190 billion per year, insurance fraud costs more than $85 billion per year, securities theft and fraud $40 billion per year, credit card and check fraud at least $13 billion per year, and cellular phone fraud about $1 billion per year.[3] Further, David Friedrichs claims that health care fraud costs Americans as much as $100 billion per year (we reported $80 billion in losses in chapter 1), and that more than 10 percent of the total health care costs in the country are due to fraud.[4] Medicare and Medicaid fraud is also widespread, costing Americans tens of billions of dollars each year. This fraud not only leads to financial losses but also "drains off medical resources, deprives patients of needed care, and in some cases leads to direct injury of patients through unnecessary and harmful operations."[5] Another form of fraud, telemarketing fraud, costs Americans losses in the tens of billions of dollars every year (in chapter 1 we reported losses of $40 billion per year).[6] And recall from chapter 1 that securities and commodities fraud costs Americans another $40 billion every year.

Another form of fraud is *quackery*, which consists of selling worthless medical products, including devices, drugs, and even nutritional products. Quackery costs consumers tens of billions of dollars in losses every year.[7] According to David Simon, unnecessary medical tests cost Americans hundreds of billions of dollars each year.[8] This form of fraud is obviously widespread.

Fraud is quite common in certain types of businesses. For example, the Federal Trade Commission asserted that nearly one-third of all money spent on auto repairs was fraudulent, meaning that Americans lose about $60 million every day on automotive fraud.[9] Other repair service industries are also notorious for committing fraud against their customers.[10] According to Stephen Rosoff and colleagues, "Much of the auto repair fraud that has been uncovered implicates major corporate chains, whose stature and public trust are far removed from fly-by-night garages."[11] This fact reminds us that crimes like fraud are normal in the context of big business.

Many "diet and nutrition" companies, such as Diet Centers, NordicTrack, Jenny Craig, Nutri/System, Physicians Weight Loss Centers, and SlimAmerica, have been held accountable for different forms of fraud. Their activities generally revolve around making false or misleading claims, something to be discussed later in this chapter.[12]

Typically, the most vulnerable are often targeted, including the poor and elderly. Rosoff and colleagues explain: "Fraudulent loan companies purchase lists of persons experiencing hard times, such as those involved in foreclosure proceedings, and either telephone them or mail them loan applications guaranteeing approval in exchange for upfront fees."[13] Additionally, recent evidence shows similar activity by credit card companies, leading to major increases in personal bankruptcy filings,[14] as well as by banks, leading to the record level of home foreclosures seen nationwide.[15] Once again, these are typically large, respectable corporations involved in such behavior.

The Credit Learning Center reports that "credit card companies are being accused of predatory marketing and business practices. Marketing risk managers for credit card companies often target the young, the poor, and most vulnerable consumers for their offers."[16] Table 4.1 illustrates some of the practices major credit card companies have allegedly used.

According to the National Consumer Law Center (NCLC): "Millions of consumers are being victimized by "credit" card offers that charge hundreds

Table 4.1. Alleged Practices of Major Credit Card Companies

Terms and conditions that are not made available to potential customers are hard to find by applicants.
High-pressure sales tactics by new application representatives.
Penalties that increase interest rates dramatically when you pay your bill late just once.
Very high late fees and "tiered" late fees (which vary according to the balance).
Hourly "cut off times" on top of normal due dates.
Over limit fees.
Deceptive interest rate quotes.
Extremely high cash advance fees.
Card inactivity fees.

Source: Credit Learning Center. Why are credit card companies coming under intense fire? Retrieved from www.creditlearningcenter.com/display.php?content_id=36.

of dollars in fees and extend minimal available credit—sometimes as little as $50. These cards . . . share a common thread: high fees that eat up most of an already low credit limit, leaving the consumer with little real, useable credit and at a high price." One example provided by NCLC shows how it works. One credit card comes with a credit limit of $250; yet, consumers who apply for the card will "incur a $95 program fee, a $29 account set-up fee, a $6 monthly participation fee, and a $48 annual fee—an instant debt of $178 and buying power of only $72."[17]

As for the recent "mortgage crisis" that has hit America hard, the Community Investment Network (CIN) explains that the "American dream of homeownership is being seriously threatened by a segment of the nation's mortgage lenders and brokers who are utilizing a variety of abusive lending practices to cheat, exploit and strip away the home equity (value) from individual homeowners and in some cases the equity of entire communities." CIN asserts that unscrupulous companies, "cloaked in a mantle of 'trust,' . . . engage in predatory lending practices that are questionable, fraudulent, and in many case just plain illegal."[18] Predatory mortgage loans are actually designed to exploit vulnerable populations and are characterized by heavy interest and fees and abusive terms and conditions "that trap borrowers and lead to a spiral of increased indebtedness."[19] Typically these loans are aimed at the poor, women, and people of color, and they generally are not at all concerned with the borrower's ability to repay the loan.[20]

According to CIN: "The main targets of predatory mortgage lenders are families and individuals with less than perfect credit histories. These persons have limited incomes, but do have equity (value) in their homes, and historically have been the elderly, minorities and women. They are frequently individuals whose homes are in need of repair, or homes that have been damaged as a result of natural disasters such as hurricanes, tornados or floods. In most, but not all cases, they are ineligible for 'normal' prime mortgage loans and must go to sub-prime loan lenders (loans offered at very high interest rates to people with bad credit ratings)."[21] Table 4.2 illustrates some of the practices used by banks.

Why do credit card companies and banks engage in such activity? Because it is very profitable! For example, the company CompuCredit collected hundreds of million of dollars in fees "from a portfolio of fee-harvester cards that by mid-2007 had saddled cardholders with nearly $1 billion in debt."[22] And the wealthiest of the wealthy individuals and banks have "earned" tens of billions of dollars through such fraudulent practices.[23]

As we suggested in chapter 3, the desire to make money, regardless of how much is already being earned by corporations, takes precedence over every other concern, even morality. Perhaps that explains why even babies and their

Table 4.2.   Alleged Practices of Major Banks

Marketing
1. Aggressive solicitations to targeted neighborhoods—Companies typically advertise through television commercials, direct mail, by telephone and door to door. The companies use terms like "no credit, no problem," or "credit never a problem." They frequently distribute live checks, that when endorsed and cashed commit homeowners to high interest, high fee, second mortgages putting their homeownership at risk.
2. Home improvement scams—Predatory mortgage lenders use local home improvement companies to solicit loan business. The home improvement contractor makes claims that are frequently untruthful including stating the government will pay for a portion of the repairs. Repairs are done without the necessary permits, and the homeowner is often overcharged for the work.
3. Kickbacks to mortgage brokers ("Yield Spread Premiums")—While pretending to work for the homeowner to find them the "best" mortgage, the broker is actually working for the predatory lender and receives fees from the homeowner and also the predatory mortgage company for bringing them new business.
4. Racial steering to high rate lenders—Minority homeowners who would be eligible for prime loans (some studies indicated at least 50 percent), if they approached the right financial institution, fall victim to brokers and others who steer them to predatory subprime lenders where fees and profits are higher.

Sales Procedures
1. Purposely structuring loans with payments the borrower cannot afford—Loans should be structured on the borrower's ability to pay, not on whether the house value can "cover" the amount of the loan.
2. Falsifying loan applications (particularly income level)—Lenders pretend to assist homeowners to secure a mortgage by falsifying income levels, but in reality they help cause financial hardship and possible calamity for the borrower.
3. Adding insincere cosigners—Lenders/brokers add individuals who do not have any will, ability, or the money to support the payment of the loan in order to secure the mortgage.
4. Making loans to mentally incapacitated homeowners.
5. Forging signatures on loan documents (i.e., required disclosure)—Salesmen are forging borrowers' signatures to documents that place the borrowers' home in jeopardy, or ask the borrowers to sign applications that have blank spaces that are filled in later with higher rates and fees than agreed upon.
6. Encouraging borrowers to pay off lower income mortgages—Lenders urge borrowers to pay off lower income mortgages and then replace them with larger mortgages with higher rates.
7. Shifting unsecured debt into mortgages—Lenders counsel borrowers to pay off credit card debts or health costs with second mortgages.
8. Offering loans in excess of 100 percent LTV [loan to value]—Lenders offer a loan on your house that is more than its value.
9. Changing the loan terms at closing—This tactic causes higher fees and higher loan payments and violates many state laws on full disclosure of mortgage details before closing.

The Loan Itself
1. High annual interest rates—All rates should be in line with other subprime rates being charged by other financial institutions.

(continues)

Table 4.2. (*continued*)

2. High points or padded closing costs.
3. Balloon payments—Loans that require a huge payment within three to eight years, a payment so high that it would require a new loan.
4. Inflated appraisal costs—A major cause of foreclosures when the home is appraised way beyond its actual value and the amount of the mortgage is then increased.
5. Padded recording fees—Fees above what is set by local and state laws.
6. Bogus broker fees—Fees in excess of those set by law and/or industry.
7. Unbundling (itemizing duplicate services and charging separately for then)— Charging one fee for several un-itemized services, and then itemizing the services and charging for each of them *again.*
8. Required credit insurance—Requiring borrower to pay for credit insurance to guard against a default, sometimes requiring it to be prepaid and placed as part of the loan; borrower then has to pay interest on the insurance premium.
9. Falsely identified loans as "lines of credit" or "open end mortgages."
10. Forced placed homeowners insurance—Requiring homeowners insurance supplied by lender or mortgage broker, sometimes requiring it to be prepaid and placed as part of the loan; borrower then has to pay interest on the insurance premium.
11. Mandatory arbitration clauses—Borrower waves right to take lender to court regarding the mortgage; requires arbitration in location and by individuals hired by the lender.

After Closing
1. Flipping (repeated refinancing, often after high-pressure sales)—This repeated refinancing usually has no benefit to the homeowner in lower rates or shorter time frame for payment. It generates higher fees, higher rates, and more profit for the lender . . . and nothing but grief for the borrower.
2. Charging daily interest when loan payments are late—There is usually a ten to fifteen day grace period before late payments are charged and late payments are usually based on weeks, not a daily calculation.
3. Engaging in abusive collection practices—Garnishment of wages without due process, phone calls and visits, and the threatening of borrowers are frequent occurrences.
4. Charging excessive prepayment penalties—Setting excessive charges so that paying off the loan early becomes too costly, and borrowers are stuck paying the loan and all the interest over the entire agreed upon period.
5. Engaging in foreclosure abuses—Lenders move to foreclose too quickly and sell the house (or buy the house themselves) far below market value to cover the loan; both actions leave the homeowner with nothing.
6. Failing to report good payment on borrowers' credit reports—By failing to report good payment activity, borrowers' credit never improves and lenders can continue to loan them funds at subprime rates.
7. Failing to provide accurate loan balance and payoff amount—This action works to discourage payoff of loan and thereby avoid a loss of interest to lender; inaccurate information causes the borrower to pay more than necessary to satisfy the loan.

Source: Community Investment Network. Predatory mortgage lending overview. Retrieved from www.com-munityinvestmentnetwork.org/single-news-item-states/article/predatory-mortgage-lending-overview/?tx_tt news%5BbackPid%5D=1027&cHash=93dc37f04d.

parents are targets of fraud. One well-known example of such deceptive practices is the Beech-Nut Corporation which admitted to 215 counts of shipping containers of beet sugar, cane sugar syrup, corn syrup, water, flavoring, and coloring, marketed as "pure apple juice."[24]

There are numerous well-known corporate crimes that have involved significant, high-level frauds. The 1980s and 1990s gave us the savings and loan (S&L) scandals, which cost Americans hundreds of billions of dollars in losses, and the late 1990s and early twenty-first century gave us the stories of Enron, WorldCom, and other major corporations that defrauded Americans of additional hundreds of billions of dollars.

S&Ls (also known as "thrifts") were created in the 1930s to help people build homes during the Great Depression. According to Jeffrey Reiman: "The system had built into it important limitations on the kinds of loans that could be made and was subject to federal supervision to prevent the bank failures that came in the wake of the Depression of 1929."[25] Yet, beginning in the 1970s, efforts were made to deregulate the S&Ls. These efforts were greatly stepped up in the 1980s. The ultimate result was the collapse of scores of S&Ls, causing losses between $200 billion and $1.4 trillion![26]

What led to the collapse of so many S&Ls? One significant factor was *deregulation*, as noted in chapter 3.[27] While some may see the S&L scandals as resulting from individual greed and fraud, institutional and structural factors such as deregulation of financial industries were also involved.[28] Rosoff and colleagues explain: "Although policy-makers had gradually loosened the restraints on S&L since the early 1970s, it was not until the *laissez-faire* fervor of the early Reagan administration that this approach gained widespread political acceptance as a solution to the rapidly escalating S&L crisis. In a few strokes, Washington dismantled most of the regulatory infrastructure that had kept the thrift industry together for four decades. These deregulators were convinced that the free enterprise system works best if left alone, unhampered by perhaps well-meaning but ultimately counterproductive government controls."[29]

The net effect of deregulation is explained by Davita Glasberg and Dan Skidmore. Deregulation amounted to "far fewer field supervisors and auditors, and thus much less oversight of the financial status and practices of the savings and loans. In the absence of adequate and regular oversight, fraud became not only possible but also standard operating procedure. Deregulation of banking . . . created conditions that made widespread and regular fraudulent practices the norm."[30] Kitty Calavita and Henry Pontell assert that "collective embezzlement" in the S&L industry became standard operating procedure.[31]

The laws passed by Congress and subsequent deregulation efforts that were put into place (such as raising the amount of federally guaranteed insurance on savings accounts from $40,000 to $100,000 and allowing S&Ls to pursue riskier loans) are probably better understood as "unregulation" rather than "deregulation."[32] Francis Cullen and colleagues conclude that, because of such changes, "S&Ls were now able to induce an infusion of money by offering high interest rates and the promise of federal insurance for deposits up to $100,000—in short, a high return on a no-risk investment. As money poured in and with little oversight by banking regulators, the S&Ls attracted many unscrupulous executives seeking to 'get rich quick.' These officials not only made irresponsibly poor investments but also engaged in criminal activities, such as arranging for kickbacks on loans and the outright theft of funds—monies often used to support lavish lifestyles."[33]

Clearly, criminality played a major role in the failures of the S&Ls. Perhaps this is why the U.S. Department of Justice called the scandal an "unconscionable plundering of America's financial institutions."[34] Estimates of the amount of damage caused by criminality in the S&L scandal range from 10 percent to 80 percent, but scholars agree that it is likely that more than half of the damage was caused by various forms of elite deviance.[35] David Simon estimates that 60 percent of the total money lost through the S&L scandals was due to fraud,[36] and Jeffrey Reiman asserts that 70 to 80 percent of the failures resulted at least in part due to fraud.[37]

Rosoff and colleagues conclude, based on a federally funded study of the S&L scandals, that "crime and deliberate fraud were extensive in the thrift industry during the 1980s, thereby contributing to the collapse of hundreds of institutions and increasing the cost of the taxpayer bailout."[38] The types of frauds involved included "desperation dealing," "collective embezzlement," and "covering up." *Desperation dealing* involves making risky investments in hopes of striking it rich. If the investments paid off, large sums of money could be earned; if they did not, taxpayers would be forced to pay back the losses. *Collective embezzlement* is simply looting, or funneling money from bank accounts into personal accounts.[39]

Rosoff and colleagues suggest that, although collective embezzlement is a form of white-collar crime rather than corporate crime, it can also be considered "deviance by the organization." They explain: "Not only are the perpetrators themselves in management positions, but the very goals of the institution are to provide a money machine for owners and other insiders. The formal goals of the organization thus comprise a 'front' for the real goals of management, who not infrequently purchased the institution in order to loot it, then discard it after it serves its purpose."[40]

Further, the S&L scandals occurred because of "enablers," including appraisers, accountants, and lawyers whose "services made many of the S&L scams possible. Perhaps foremost in this regard were accountants, whose audits allowed many fraudulent transactions to go unnoticed. Professional accounting firms were highly paid for their services, and thus could easily turn a blind eye when evidence of wrongdoing surfaced."[41] One primary enabler was the U.S. government. David Friedrichs explains: "Numerous government officials helped create the circumstances that made the S&L-related crimes possible; failed to act against the thrifts as they were being mismanaged and looted, or interfered with those who should have been taking action; minimized the dimensions of the problem for a long time; and failed to take timely and effective action to respond to the crisis."[42]

In the past ten years, corporate crime shook the United States again. Next to the terrorist attacks of September 11, 2001, and the subsequent "war on terror" launched by President George W. Bush, the story of corporate crime was the biggest story of the first decade of the twentieth century. Jeffrey Reiman concurs, writing that "2002's big crime story was a long and complicated saga of corporate financial shenanigans that caused a significant drop in stock market prices."[43]

Dozens of corporations were accused of various kinds of corporate crimes such as fraud, including Arthur Andersen, Enron, WorldCom, Qwest, Tyco, ImClone, Global Crossing, Dynegy, CMS Energy, El Paso Corp., Halliburton, Williams Cos., AOL Time Warner, Goldman Sachs, Salomon Smith Barney, Citigroup, J.P. Morgan Chase, Schering Plough, Bristol-Myers Squibb, Kmart, Johnson & Johnson, Adelphia, Merrill Lynch, Rite Aid, and Coca-Cola.[44] According to *Fortune* magazine, the corporations involved were led by individuals who were "getting immensely, extraordinarily, obscenely wealthy."[45]

Many of these corporations were accused of the same basic fraudulent activities—essentially "cooking the books" in order to inflate profits by hiding debts so that investors would be more likely to invest money in the corporations. Many of the corporations treated debts as revenue in order to make them look more profitable. Think of it this way—imagine you wanted to get a loan from your local bank and you treated every check that you wrote in the past month not as debts against your account but as payments made to you by the companies you sent the checks to—this is what many companies in the United States did. Table 4.3 illustrates some of the cases against major corporations.

The cases of Enron and WorldCom have probably been the most analyzed. Enron was the seventh largest company in the United States and its stock was worth nearly $91 per share in August 2000. By late 2001, the stock's value was less than $1 per share. Enron's collapse caused the loss of $60 billion on the stock market, more than $2 billion in pension plans, and 5,600 jobs.[46] Enron ended up with debts over $31 billion and thus filed for bankruptcy protection in December 2001.[47]

Table 4.3. Alleged Crimes of Major American Corporations

AOL Time Warner—Investigated by the Security and Exchange Commission (SEC) and the Justice Department for questionable accounting practices at the company's America Online unit in 2000 and 2001.

Arthur Andersen—Found guilty of obstructing justice for shredding Enron documents and received the maximum sentence of a $500,000 fine and five years' probation. This firm also served as the accounting agency for other numerous companies accused of crimes.

Bristol-Myers Squibb—Drugmaker restated sales by $2 billion, and federal regulators investigated whether it purposely inflated sales by offering incentives to wholesalers.

Citigroup—Financial services company agreed to pay $240 million to settle "predatory lending" charges in the largest consumer protection settlement in the history of the Federal Trade Commission (FTC). It was also charged with helping Enron manipulate its finances to deceive investors.

Credit Suisse First Boston Corporation—Agreed to pay $100 million for taking millions of dollars from customers through inflated commissions in exchange for allocations of "hot" initial public offerings.

Enron—Large energy company accused of obscuring its finances with business partnerships (invented companies to hide debts) and questionable accounting practices that fooled debt-rating agencies, Wall Street analysts, and investors. Enron was forced to file for bankruptcy, causing billions in dollars of losses for investors and Enron employees, many of whose company retirement accounts became worthless. Many Enron rivals (including Dynergy, El Paso Corp., CMS Energy, Halliburton, and Williams Cos.) were also under investigation because of questionable accounting and trading activities. The Halliburton case concerned an accounting practice introduced at the company when it was headed by now Vice President Dick Cheney.

Global Crossing—Telecommunications company investigated for using "swap deals" with other telecom carriers to inflate sales. The company was suspected of selling capacity on its fiber-optic network to other carriers and then buying back a like amount, which is improper. Global Crossing filed for Chapter 11 bankruptcy protection and agreed to sell a majority stake in its fiber-optic network to two Asian investors for about $250 million in cash.

Goldman Sachs—Investment bank asked to turn over documents to the House of Representatives, which was investigating potential conflicts of interest and the distribution of stock as companies went public.

ImClone—Former CEO was convicted on charges of insider trading for allegedly trying to sell his stock and tipping off family members after learning the federal Food and Drug Administration (FDA) would refuse to review the company's application for promising cancer drug Erbitux.

Johnson & Johnson—Investigated by the FDA for false recordkeeping at a plant that makes an anemia drug linked to serious side effects.

J.P. Morgan Chase—Charged with helping Enron with $8 billion in financial dealings that made Enron look rich in cash rather than heavily indebted.

Kmart—Major retailer filed for Chapter 11 bankruptcy protection. It was investigated for an illegal loan as well as for its accounting practices (overstating profits) by the FBI and the SEC and hundreds of stores were closed and twenty-two thousand jobs were cut.

Merrill Lynch—Wall Street brokerage firm agreed to pay $100 million to settle charges from New York that its research analysts knowingly promoted stocks they privately ridiculed in order to win business for Merrill's investment banking unit.

Qwest—Telecommunications company investigated by the Securities and Exchange Commission after admitting that it had improperly accounted for about $1.2 billion in revenue for part of 2000 and all of 2001, most of it from "swap deals" it made with other companies. It restated $950 million in revenue derived from making sales to other carriers and then buying back a similar amount.

Rite Aid—Three former executives and one suspended executive of this drug store company were indicted on charges that they cooked the books to make it appear more profitable. It restated results going back three years.

Tyco—Former CEO and former CFO were charged with looting $600 million from the company. Tyco sued its former CEO for at least $730 million.

Xerox—Forced to restate earnings to reflect $1.4 billion less in pretax profits over the past five years as part of a settlement with the SEC. It was forced to pay a $10 million penalty.

WorldCom—Now known as MCI, filed the largest bankruptcy in US history. It admitted that it overstated profits by hiding more than $7 billion in expenses over five quarters. Several former WorldCom executives were charged and others pleaded guilty.

Enron's fraudulent activities can be classified as a "disinformation campaign" because it all amounted to "hiding its degree of indebtedness from investors by treating loans as revenue, and hiding company losses by creating new firms with company capital and then attributing losses to them rather than Enron."[48] To make matters worse, Enron CEO Kenneth Lay sold off $103 million of his company stock while discouraging and even forbidding his employees from selling theirs, even as the value of the stock plummeted from $80 per share to only $.30 per share. Roughly twenty thousand employees lost their retirement accounts.[49] Enron also intentionally manipulated California's power crisis for financial gain,[50] something that ultimately led to the recall of the state's governor and the subsequent election of Arnold Schwarzenegger to the position of governor.[51]

WorldCom's stock fell from a high of $64 per share to only $.09 per share. WorldCom's fraud was in the amount of $11 billion, and caused losses in the area of $180 billion as well as thirty thousand lost jobs.[52] After WorldCom was hit with a record fine for its fraud, the company changed its name and remains in business today.

Such corporations were assisted in their wrongdoings by consulting firms such as Arthur Andersen, who helped the companies hide their debts by first being their accountants and then by destroying evidence during the subsequent investigations. Interestingly, Arthur Andersen also had long ago been involved in the failing of perhaps the most infamous S&L—Charles Keating's Lincoln Savings and Loan.

The corporations were also assisted by major banks including J.P. Morgan Chase and Citigroup.[53] The *Wall Street Journal* called the banks "Enron Enablers" and wrote: "They appear to have behaved in a guileful way and helped their corporate clients undertake unsavory practices. And they appear to have had an entire division that, among other things, helped corporations avoid taxes and manipulate their balance sheets through something called structured finance, which is a huge profit center for each bank."[54] Further, brokerage firms such as Merrill Lynch saw their employees knowingly promoting the nearly worthless stocks of these corporations.

Other major corporations also engaged in similar activity. For example, Adelphia was charged by the Securities and Exchange Commission (SEC) with "fraudulently excluding $2.3 billion in debt from its earnings report. AES, AOL-Time Warner, Cedent, Halliburton, K-Mart, Lucent Technologies, MicroStrategy, Rite Aid, and Waste Management are all said to have misstated revenues in different ways at more than $100 million in each case."[55]

The total combined harms of these corporate crimes are unknown, but estimates are in the hundreds of billions of dollars if not more. David Simon asserts that "collectively, the 2002–2003 scandals helped cause a $5 trillion loss in stock market values, and cost the public at least $200 billion and one million jobs."[56] Whatever the actual harms, there is no doubt that the financial harms exceed those caused by street crime in any year by dozens of times (and numerous people have committed suicide as a result of losing all their money and/or killed their spouses and family members as a result of the stress of losing their jobs).

Keep in mind that these corporations are not nameless, faceless entities. Each is run by chief executive officers (CEOs), chief financial officers (CFOs), and a board of directors—in other words, real people who made real decisions and who can be held accountable for their actions. Some were held accountable for these frauds, but most were not. ImClone's CEO, Sam Waksal, was sentenced to eighty-seven months in prison for his role in an insider trading scandal that has shed negative light on Martha Stewart. Waksal pleaded guilty to obstruction of justice, perjury, bank fraud, and sales tax evasion. He also was sentenced to pay a fine of $3 million and more than $1.2 million in restitution. Enron founder Kenneth Lay was convicted of fraud and conspiracy but then died in July 2006 and had his convictions overturned due to being unable to appeal them. Former Enron CEO Jeffrey Skilling was sentenced to more than twenty-four years in prison for nine counts of fraud, conspiracy, insider trading, and lying to auditors, and also was ordered to pay $50 million in restitution to victims. Former Enron CFO Andrew Fastow received a sentence of six years. Interestingly, Enron paid its senior executives more than $744 million in cash and stock in the year prior to its bankruptcy filing in December 2001![57]

Most of the implicated companies simply paid fines to get out of trouble. For example, WorldCom was fined $750 million to settle the case against it, an alarmingly high figure. Yet considering that investors lost $175 billion because of WorldCom, the company was charged only about 0.4 percent of the amount of financial harm they caused. Imagine going to a bank and robbing it of $100,000 and being forced to pay back only 0.4 percent of it (which is $400)! As noted earlier, WorldCom changed its name and continues to do business, including in the rebuilding effort in Iraq.

The banks that were involved with illegal loans to help these corporations hide their losses and the accounting firms that oversaw them and turned a blind eye each faced their own investigations. One notable example is that federal and state regulators settled with ten Wall Street investment firms (including Citigroup, Merrill Lynch, J.P. Morgan Chase, and Credit Suisse First Boston) for knowingly pushing bad stocks, for conducting and publishing flawed research, and for conflicts of interest. They agreed to pay $1.4 billion in fines and to separate their investment banking activities and research activities. Most of these firms did not admit guilt and some changed their names to distance themselves from these scandals.

Although the cases of the S&Ls and the "corporate bandits" captured widespread media attention and thus are well-known to many Americans, the typical form of corporate fraud is mostly unknown. In fact, there are entire industries built on fraud. A few that come to mind are the corporations that make creams that "remove the appearance" of cellulite and stretch marks, "ab cruncher" machines, as well as many so-called health foods.

For these businesses, fraud seems to be their business. Some examples provided by Stephen Rosoff, Henry Pontell, and Robert Tillman include "adoption agencies" that collect money with no intention of providing children for their clients, "loan companies" who target the poor and collect up-front fees and never deliver the loans, "investment brokers" who collect money from people based on religion or other connections, and "land developers" who entice the elderly into investing money into retirement properties that are virtually worthless or uninhabitable.[58] Other fraudulent companies collect payments for the promise of lucrative modeling contracts for children; sell songs or music written by their scam victims, or publish their books, without giving credit or paying the original owners; promote others' inventions as their own; fraudulently receive winnings from a lottery or a will; and so forth.[59] Additionally, widely known frauds are committed by home improvement and land sale companies, travel and time-share companies, employment and telemarketing agencies, consumer debt companies, and many others.

How Fraud Involves Maximization

Maximization involves the simultaneous utilization of legitimate and illegitimate means in pursuit of the American Dream. That is, people engage in maximization when they violate the law (or engage in deviant behaviors) in the context of work (a form of conformity). Since most forms of fraud are committed in the context of work, it is a perfect example of maximization.

Businesses are, by definition, utilizing legitimate means of opportunity in pursuit of wealth. This is conformity. When businesses are also involved in fraudulent activity, the fraud is considered a form of innovation, whereby the business has invented an illegal and/or deviant means of achieving wealth. In that businesses utilize fraud as part of normal business practice, this is maximization.

When a company creates, markets, and sells a product, that is a legal activity protected and encouraged by the criminal law (conformity). If the company promotes a product it knows does not work properly or perform as advertised, or if any other deceit or trickery is involved in the property trans-action (innovation)—this is maximization.

Selling products that simply do not work is a good example of maximi-zation. Creams that claim to reduce the appearance of stretch marks or the appearance of cellulite do not claim to actually remove stretch marks or cel-lulite, only "the appearance of" stretch marks or cellulite. Consumers who do not read the labels carefully (or at all) are often misled by the claims of the manufacturers of these products. The manufacturers of the products know full well they are not effective, yet sell them anyway. Likewise, companies that sell products that supposedly help people lose weight are technically involved in a legal activity (conformity). Since such products don't work, we can see them as examples of maximization—using illegitimate or deviant means in conjunction with normal business activity.

Many may react to such business with the claim that it should be illegal (and it probably should). However, selling such products *is* legal, and therefore it is *not* an example of innovation. Further, the sale of such products is actually protected by the law, as long as the manufacturers do not claim the product actually works to reduce stretch marks or cellulite, or as long as they add a statement to the effect of: "These claims have not been analyzed by the Food and Drug Administration." In essence, American consumers are expected to protect themselves from deceptive activities under the principle of *caveat emptor* (let the buyer beware) and *laissez-faire* economics (the doctrine of government noninterference in business).[60] The former doctrine suggests that if you get ripped off by fraudulent salespeople it is your own fault; you should have known better. The latter doctrine suggests that the government has no legitimate role in regulating business, as explained in chapter 3.

Advertising a wide variety of "ab cruncher" machines is very similar. These machines—involving some form of modified sit-up workout—when used in conjunction with proper diet and a full exercise regime that involves an intense aerobic component (e.g., jogging or swimming) can lead to a slimmer, stronger, more muscular physique. Used in isolation, such machines only strengthen one's midsection. Sure enough, if a person uses these machines, he or she may develop stronger abdominal muscles. Yet, if the person does not eat a healthy, balanced diet and burn more calories than he or she consumes through intense exercise, the stronger abs will remain hidden under pounds of stomach fat. The physique of the models that are being used to sell such products is not reasonably attained by the average person (since genetics also plays an important role). Further, it is a virtual certainty that the models regularly engage in intense exercise above and beyond the "ab cruncher" approach. Finally, fitness experts assert that such ab machines are completely unnecessary since traditional abdominal exercises such as crunches performed on the floor without any equipment are highly effective.

The companies that promote these products are not engaged in any illegal activity and are careful to point out that results shown in the ads "are not typical." They also say, in some format, that the "ab cruncher" machine only works when used in conjunction with a comprehensive program of proper nutrition (i.e., diet) and regular aerobic exercise. The fraud is thus not explicit but rather implicit in the claim that one can "rock their way" or "roll their way" or "rock and roll their way" to better fitness with an ab cruncher machine. Businesses that sell these products are engaged in legitimate business (conformity) but simultaneously are using deviant means (i.e., fraud or deceptive advertising) to maximize their wealth (innovation). This is maximization.

Deceptive Advertising

Defined

According to David Simon: "One tenet of capitalism is expansion. Every corporation wishes to produce an increasing amount so that profits likewise will inflate. The problem, of course, is that the public must be convinced to consume this ever larger surplus. One way to create demand is through advertising."[61]

Advertising is obviously an expense incurred by corporations. Since corporations are in the business of making money, logic suggests that corporations do not like to waste money on advertisements that do not work. Further, corporations employ the top marketing experts to design effective ads on sample markets and focus groups prior to using them on mass audiences. Given this, one can assume that all advertisements are intended to do exactly what they do. That is, if advertisements induce young people to try and use products (even illegal ones such as tobacco and alcohol), it is logical to assume that this is the intent of the advertisements. Further, if advertisements are deceptive, it is logical to assume they are intended to be misleading.

Deceptive advertising is a form of fraud whereby a product is sold using false or misleading claims. That is, deceptive advertising is a form of theft where people willingly part with their money because of false or misleading claims about a product they purchased. A business can be held liable for false advertising if advertising for their products has the potential to deceive, even if the advertisement is not intended to deceive.

False advertising can be distinguished from mere "puffery" — advertisements that feature "self-serving ballyhoo or irrelevant celebrity endorsements."[62] A recent approach by companies misleads consumers by using actors who have played well-known fictional characters on television to endorse related professional services (e.g., an actor who has played a lawyer on a television show pitches a group of law firms). According to David Simon, puffery is legal even though the intent is to mislead: "The goal, as is always the case with advertising, is to use whatever means will sell the product. If that includes trifling with the truth, then so be it."[63] Ford's slogan, "Quality is Job 1," is a good example of puffery. Yet, given its historic and recent troubles with defective automobiles, one wonders how the company can get away with using such a slogan. In chapter 5, we will present some examples of defective products.

According to the Federal Trade Commission (FTC), which has oversight of product advertising in the United States, the Federal Trade Commission Act states that advertising must be truthful and nondeceptive, advertisers must have evidence to back up their claims, and advertisements cannot be unfair. According to the FTC's "Deception Policy Statement,"[64] an ad is deceptive if it contains a statement (or omits information) that "is likely to mislead consumers acting reasonably" and when it is "material." It is *material* if the ad is "important to a consumer's decision to buy or use the product." For example, material claims often deal with "a product's performance, features, safety, price, or effectiveness." Finally, the FTC looks at whether advertisers can justify their claims with evidence: "The law requires that advertisers have proof before the ad runs."[65]

FTC's "Unfairness Policy Statement"[66] specifies that an ad or business practice is unfair if "it causes or is likely to cause substantial consumer injury which a consumer could not reasonably avoid" and "it is not outweighed by the benefit to consumers." Further, additional laws at the federal level apply to ads for specialized products including consumer leases, credit issues, 900 telephone numbers, and other products that are sold through mail order or telephone sales. Finally, all fifty states have similar laws aimed at protecting consumers from deceptive ads.[67]

Many see the goal of the FTC to be prevention rather than punishment. That is, the FTC is not generally interested in punishing companies for running deceptive ads. The FTC explains that when it investigates a claim of false advertising, it first "looks at the ad from the point of view of the 'reasonable consumer'—the typical person looking at the ad. Rather than focusing on certain words, the FTC looks at the ad in context—words, phrases, and pictures—to determine what it conveys to consumers." The FTC "looks at both 'express' and 'implied' claims." Express claims are those claims actually made in the ad, such as that a product will cure an illness. Implied claims are "made indirectly or by inference," such as that a product will cure an illness by killing the germs that cause that illness. According to the FTC, "advertisers must have proof to back up express *and* implied claims that consumers take from an ad."[68] The FTC also looks at what the ad does not say.

The typical sanction is to order the advertiser to stop its illegal acts, or to include disclosure of additional information that serves to avoid the chance of deception, but there are no fines or prison time except for the infrequent instances when an advertiser refuses to stop despite being ordered to do so. According to the FTC, its most common actions include cease and desist orders (ordering companies to stop running deceptive ads), civil penalties (fines), and corrective advertising (providing information to consumers about deceptive ads).

The mandate of the FTC's Bureau of Consumer Protection is "to protect consumers against unfair, deceptive or fraudulent practices." Table 4.4 illustrates the types of claims and ads that its Division of Advertising Practices— "the nation's enforcer of federal truth-in-advertising laws"—focuses on.

According to the FTC, it focuses mostly on ads that make claims about health or safety as well as ads that make claims that consumers would have trouble evaluating for themselves. Such forms of false advertising are widespread. One

Table 4.4. Focus of the Federal Trade Commission's Bureau of Consumer Protection

Claims for foods, drugs, dietary supplements, and other products promising health benefits.

Health fraud on the Internet.

Weight-loss advertising.

Advertising and marketing directed to children.

Performance claims for computers, ISPs and other high-tech products and services.

Tobacco and alcohol advertising, including monitoring for unfair practices or deceptive claims and reporting to Congress on cigarette and smokeless tobacco labeling, advertising and promotion.

Protecting children's privacy online.

Claims about product performance made in national or regional newspapers and magazines; in radio and TV commercials, including infomercials; through direct mail to consumers; or on the Internet.

Source: Federal Trade Commission. Facts for consumers. A guide to the Federal Trade Commission. Retrieved November 8, 2007, from www.ftc.gov/bcp/edu/pubs/consumer/general/gen03.shtm.

need only turn on the television or open up a newspaper to see numerous examples of false advertising. Given that false advertising can literally occur with any product, it is widespread in the United States.

Examples

False advertising occurs in television ads, radio ads, Internet ads, on websites, as well as in print ads. Typically, false advertising occurs when faulty or misleading claims are made about a product. One example is a store advertising a range of household products in a given collection (e.g., furniture) that are being placed on sale. The ad specifies that "all products" in the collection are on sale, which presumably includes the table and chairs depicted in the ad. However, the table and chairs are actually *not* on sale, even though they are part of the collection and shown in the ad. Consumers who go to buy the table and chairs at the sale price become victims of false advertising when they must pay the regular price for the products.

Other examples of false advertising include inflating the original price so as to make the sale price appear more reasonable, and "near continuous sales," where items are so regularly on sale that the sale price is really the regular price. Once again, major corporations, such as the Home Shopping Network, have been found engaging in such activities.

However, a more insidious form of false advertising is referred to as "product shrinkage." Product shrinkage occurs when less and less of a product (e.g., potato chips, baked beans, soup, toilet paper, and virtually any other product) is packaged in the same size container over time. That is, the product is shrinking whereas the size of the package is not. Here are two examples. One major company that produces tampons stopped offering forty tampons in a box and began offering only thirty-two tampons in a box (for the same price). Women noticed, complained, and ultimately the company began offering forty tampons again. However, the corporation added a label to the box, saying "Now 8 more free!" Of course, women were not getting eight free tampons, they were instead receiving the same forty that they used to receive before the company shrank the amount of the product offered to consumers. This example of product shrinkage was noticed because it was so blatant.

Typically, product shrinkage is much more subtle than this. For example, another corporation went from offering a four-pack of toilet paper that contained 400 two-ply sheets per roll to only 396 two-ply sheets per roll (meaning in a four pack, consumers would receive 16 less sheets of toilet paper, hardly noticeable). Instead of announcing that the company was providing less product for the same price, the company said nothing and instead added an additional label to its package, saying: "Now even better!" The product was exactly the same as before, only consumers would receive less product for the same price (in essence, the product *was* now even better—but only for the corporation). Usually, corporations say nothing about product shrinkage—they make no changes to their packaging other than the fine print on the back of the product that indicates how much of the product is included (e.g., how many ounces). This practice is common in virtually every product in your grocery store. It is accepted as legitimate business practice.

Product shrinkage is more common now than ever, but products have always been advertised at exaggerated sizes. David Simon provides some examples: "Lumber is uniformly shorter than advertised; a 12-inch board really is 11¼ inches wide. The quarter-pounder advertised by McDonald's is really 3⅞ ounces. Nine-inch pies are in truth 7¾ inches in diameter because the pie industry includes the rim of the pan in determining the stated size."[69] So, it appears deceptive advertising is the norm in American business.

A final example of deceptive advertising is when companies promote products that simply do not work, as discussed earlier. For instance, pills that are advertised as weight loss pills or diets that allow you to "eat as much food as you want and still lose weight." A more serious deception involves children's cough syrups. Joe Graedon and Terry Graedon write: "Parents ought to be outraged. They have been betrayed by drug companies as well as the Food and Drug Administration. For decades, the FDA has allowed hundreds of cough and cold remedies to be sold for treating kids with sniffles and coughs. These products were permitted even though there wasn't any scientific proof that they worked to help children recover more quickly or even to alleviate their symptoms." Six studies conducted since 1985 found no evidence that the products were effective. Yet, drug companies spend about $50 million every year promoting these products, claiming they are "pediatrician recommended" even though their use has actually been discouraged by the American Academy of Pediatrics! To make matters worse, the products are not only ineffective but are also potentially dangerous, causing symptoms like abnormal heart rhythm and hallucinations, unintended overdose due to interdiction effects, as well as death.[70] The FDA currently advises parents not to use these products for kids less than six years of age, but the products are still sold and marketed to parents of younger children (although some of the products were voluntarily recalled by manufacturers).[71]

How Deceptive Advertising Involves Maximization

Maximization occurs when legitimate and illegitimate means are used simultaneously in pursuit of wealth. As with fraud, deceptive advertising is committed in the context of legitimate business; therefore, it is another good example of maximization. Deceptive advertising combines conformity and innovation to try to "sell" consumers on products or services based on faulty or misleading claims. This is maximization.

When companies create, market, and sell products, this is a legal activity protected and encouraged by the criminal law (conformity). If the company makes false or misleading claims that are not backed by empirical evidence and that have the potential to mislead (innovation)—this is maximization. Even when the misleading activities are subtle, such as in the case of product shrinkage, they also involve maximization. In the case of product shrinkage, businesses are deceiving consumers to believe that they are getting the same amount of product—since it is in the same size package as before—even though the amount of product in the packaging has been reduced. This combination of normal business activity (producing and packaging foods) with deviance (shrinking the package without telling consumers) is maximization.

HOW FRAUD AND DECEPTIVE ADVERTISING ARE EXPLAINED BY CONTEXTUAL ANOMIE/STRAIN THEORY

Fraud and deceptive advertising are explained by contextual anomie/strain theory (CAST). Recall that contextual anomie/strain theory attributes criminality to a prioritization of the goals associated with the American Dream over the legitimate means to achieve those goals (Robert Merton's anomie theory); frustrations produced by goal blockage whereby individuals are unable to achieve the goals associated with the American Dream, regardless of how much they have (Merton's strain theory); a prioritization of the economy over other noneconomic institutions in America (Steven Messner and Richard Rosenfeld's institutional anomie theory); and greater presence of opportunities for deviance in some situations than in others (Richard Cloward and Lloyd Ohlin's differential opportunity theory). Further, there are additional conditions within the context of the corporation whereby individuals, groups, and subcultures are subjected to added pressures to innovate.

Fraud and deceptive advertising occur in corporations because of greed, and greed arises out of the dual pressures exerted on individuals within the corporate subculture as well as by other societal institutions that promote attainment of wealth over any and all other valuable goals. In American society, the welfare of the economy is given priority over all other institutions. The cultural goals of the American Dream are learned in schools and promoted by parents and the polity, acting as surrogates for corporate and capitalistic interests. We all, to some degree or another, subjugate our own interests in order to pursue the goals of the American Dream, even if and when it interferes with the health and happiness of our families. This creates enormous pressure on individuals to pursue the American Dream, no matter the means available for achieving it.

Clearly, these pressures are not sufficient to explain greedy behaviors such as fraud and deceptive advertising (both forms of maximization), because most people who experience societal pressures do not regularly engage in crimes like fraud and false advertising. However, these pressures do promote greedy behaviors (some of them criminal, some not) by individuals, as well as within corporations.

Our argument is that maximization occurs because of the additional pressures operating on individuals within the corporation. In corporations, the primary means of satisfying greed by elites is maximization—using illegitimate means (i.e., criminality, deviance) in conjunction with legitimate means (i.e., work). Elites simultaneously engage in innovation and conformity to achieve even greater wealth. We have shown in this chapter that maximization is accepted, expected, and even celebrated within American corporations. It is the *de facto* means of succeeding and excelling. It is, simply stated, normal.

The corporate subculture that has emerged as corporations have gained more and more strength and prominence in American society encourages and at times mandates elite deviance through maximization. Further, it provides justifications for forms of elite deviance such as fraud and deceptive advertising through maximization. Individuals neutralize their bond to societal rules as well as personal morals as they pursue the corporate mandated goal of outlandish levels of wealth.

However, it is important to keep in mind that corporate crime involves entities that promote their own interests beyond that of the individuals who make up the corporation. In this context, individual morals and values are overwhelmed by corporate interests and ultimately become irrelevant; individuals are contractually obliged to pursue the best interests of the corporation (even when they conflict with social good); loyalty to the corporation significantly impacts individual behavior; true social responsibility is illegal; and over time, legitimate and illegitimate means of pursuing wealth and the American Dream become blurred and simply unimportant.

We expect maximization to be prevalent in American corporations. This is not only because it is so celebrated within corporations, but also because corporate managers tend to have personality traits (such as desire for control) that make maximization more likely. Further, maximization is more likely due to its high rewards, low levels of regulation of business, small likelihood of punishment for wrongdoing, and degree of reward (e.g., financial raise). Finally, maximization is very common because opportunities for it are so immense. Crime is rampant in corporations because they are organized for the concomitant implementation of legitimate and illegitimate means in pursuit of wealth.

NOTES

1. Mokhiber, Russell (2007). Twenty things you should know about corporate crime. Retrieved September 21, 2007, from www.commondreams.org/archive/2007/06/13/1859/.

2. Friedrichs, David (2006). *Trusted Criminals: White Collar Crime in Contemporary Society* (3rd ed.). Belmont, CA: Wadsworth, 85.

3. Reiman, Jeffrey (2006). *The Rich Get Richer and the Poor Get Prison* (8th ed.). Boston, MA: Allyn & Bacon, 117.

4. Friedrichs, *Trusted Criminals*, 85.

5. Friedrichs, *Trusted Criminals*, 104.

6. Rosoff, Stephen, Henry Pontell, and Robert Tillman (2002). *Profit Without Honor: White-Collar Crime and the Looting of America* (2nd ed.). Upper Saddle River, NJ: Prentice Hall, 49.

7. Rosoff, Pontell, and Tillman, *Profit Without Honor*, 117, 120–21.

8. Simon, David (2006). *Elite Deviance* (8th ed.). Boston, MA: Allyn & Bacon, 121.

9. Rosoff, Pontell, and Tillman, *Profit Without Honor*, 46.

10. Friedrichs, *Trusted Criminals*, 99.

11. Rosoff, Pontell, and Tillman, *Profit Without Honor*, 47.

12. Simon, *Elite Deviance*, 117; Rosoff, Pontell, and Tillman, *Profit Without Honor*, 58.

13. Rosoff, Pontell, and Tillman, *Profit Without Honor*, 54.

14. Consumer Law Center (2007). Fee-harvesters: Low-credit, high-cost cards bleed consumers. Retrieved January 24, 2008, from www.nclc.org/issues/credit_cards/content/FEE-HarvesterFinal.pdf.

15. Community Investment Network (2006). Predatory mortgage lending overview. Retrieved January 24, 2008, from www.communityinvestmentnetwork.org/single-news-item-states/article/predatory-mortgage-lending-overview/?tx_ttnews%5BbackPid%5D=1027&cHash=93dc37f04d.

16. Credit Learning Center (2008). Why are credit card companies coming under intense fire? Retrieved January 24, 2008, from www.creditlearningcenter.com/display.php?content_id=36.

17. Credit Learning Center, Why are credit card companies coming under intense fire?

18. Community Investment Network, Predatory mortgage lending overview.

19. Community Investment Network, Predatory mortgage lending overview.

20. Community Investment Network, Predatory mortgage lending overview.

21. Community Investment Network, Predatory mortgage lending overview.

22. Credit Learning Center, Why are credit card companies coming under intense fire?

23. Lord, Richard (2004). *American Nightmare: Predatory Lending and the Foreclosure of the American Dream*. Monroe, ME: Common Courage Press; Squires, Gregory (2004). *Why the Poor Pay More: How to Stop Predatory Lending*. Westport, CT: Praeger.

24. Simon, *Elite Deviance*, 121.

25. Reiman, *The Rich Get Richer*, 139.

26. Rosoff, Pontell, and Tillman, *Profit Without Honor*, 268.

27. Simon, *Elite Deviance*, 48–49.

28. Glasberg, Davita, and Dan Skidmore (1998). The role of the state in the criminogenesis of corporate crime: A case study of the savings and loan crisis. *Social Science Quarterly* 79(1): 110–28.

29. Rosoff, Pontell, and Tillman, *Profit Without Honor*, 269.

30. Glasberg and Skidmore, The role of the state in the criminogenesis of corporate crime: A case study of the savings and loan crisis. *Social Science Quarterly* 79(1): 111.

31. Calavita, Kitty, and Henry Pontell (1990). "Heads I win, tails you lose": Deregulation, crime, and crisis in the savings and loan industry. *Crime and Delinquency* 36(3): 309–41.

32. Rosoff, Pontell, and Tillman, *Profit Without Honor*, 271.

33. Cullen, Francis, Gray Cavender, William Maakestad, and Michael Benson (2006). *Corporate Crime Under Attack: The Fight to Criminalize Business Violence.* Cincinnati, OH: Anderson, 21.

34. Cullen et al., *Corporate Crime Under Attack*, 21.

35. Rosoff, Pontell, and Tillman, *Profit Without Honor*, 268–69.

36. Simon, *Elite Deviance*, 51.

37. Reiman, *The Rich Get Richer*, 140.

38. Rosoff, Pontell, and Tillman, *Profit Without Honor*, 278.

39. Friedrichs, *Trusted Criminals*, 160.

40. Rosoff, Pontell, and Tillman, *Profit Without Honor*, 273.

41. Rosoff, Pontell, and Tillman, *Profit Without Honor*, 275.

42. Friedrichs, *Trusted Criminals*, 162.

43. Reiman, www.paulsjusticepage.com/RichGetRicher/fraud.htm.

44. Robinson, Matthew (2009). *Justice Blind? Ideals and Realities of American Criminal Justice* (3rd ed.). Upper Saddle River, NJ: Prentice Hall.

45. Reiman, *The Rich Get Richer*, 122.

46. Cullen et al., *Corporate Crime Under Attack*, 22.

47. Reiman, *The Rich Get Richer*, 122.

48. Reiman, *The Rich Get Richer*, 122.

49. Reiman, *The Rich Get Richer*, 122.

50. Reiman, *The Rich Get Richer*, 125.

51. Eichenwald, Curt (2005). *Conspiracy of Fools: A True Story*. Portland, OR: Broadway Books; McLean, Bethany, and Peter Elkind (2003). *Smartest Guys in the Room: The Amazing Rise and Scandalous Fall of Enron*. Portfolio Publishers; Schwartz, Mimi, and Sherron Watkins (2004). *Power Failure: The Inside Story of the Collapse of Enron*. Strawberry Hills, Australia: Currency.

52. Cullen et al., *Corporate Crime Under Attack*, 21.

53. Reiman, *The Rich Get Richer*, 123.

54. Reiman, *The Rich Get Richer*, 122.

55. Reiman, *The Rich Get Richer*, 123.

56. Simon, *Elite Deviance*, 126.

57. Robinson, *Justice Blind?*

58. Rosoff, Pontell, and Tillman, *Profit Without Honor*, 45–46.

59. Friedrichs, *Trusted Criminals*, 197.

60. Simon, David, and Frank Hagan (1999). *White-Collar Deviance*. Boston, MA: Allyn and Bacon, 158.

61. Simon, *Elite Deviance*, 116.

62. Rosoff, Pontell, and Tillman, *Profit Without Honor*, 56.

63. Simon, *Elite Deviance*, 119.

64. Federal Trade Commission (1983). FTC policy statement on deception. Retrieved November 8, 2007, from www.ftc.gov/bcp/policystmt/ad-decept.htm.

65. Federal Trade Commission (2001). Facts for Business. Frequently asked advertising questions: A guide for small business. Retrieved November 8, 2007, from www.ftc.gov/bcp/conline/pubs/buspubs/ad-faqs.shtm.

66. Federal Trade Commission (1980). FTC policy statement on unfairness. Retrieved November 8, 2007, from www.ftc.gov/bcp/policystmt/ad-unfair.htm.

67. Federal Trade Commission, Facts for Business.

68. Federal Trade Commission, Facts for Business.

69. Simon, *Elite Deviance*, 118.

70. Graedon, Joe, and Terry Graedon (2007). Cold-remedy ads fool parents. *The News & Observer*, December 23.

71. CNN (2007). FDA panel: No cold medicines to children under 6. Retrieved January 31, 2008, from www.cnn.com/2007/HEALTH/10/19/coldmed.fda/index.html.

5

Maximization and Elite Violent Crime

> The violent or "physical" costs—the toll in lives lost, injuries inflicted, and illnesses suffered—are perhaps the gravest and certainly the most neglected of the damages that corporate lawlessness imposes on the American people.
>
> —Francis Cullen, Gray Cavender, William Maakestad,
> and Michael Benson, *Corporate Crime Under Attack:*
> *The Fight to Criminalize Business Violence* (2006)[1]

When people think of corporate crime, they most likely think of corporate property crimes. However, corporate crime is also quite deadly. It kills and injures far more people every year than street crime. While there are oftentimes differences in the degree of culpability between violent street crimes and violent corporate crimes (as discussed in chapter 1), corporate violence tends to involve negligence and reckless behaviors. Thus, corporations and their executives can be and should be held accountable for their actions.

In this chapter, we apply our theory of elite deviance—*contextual anomie/strain theory*—to show how the majority of corporate violence involves maximization. Like in chapter 4, our approach in this chapter is to (1) introduce specific forms of corporate violence, describing them in detail with specific examples; (2) illustrate how these forms of elite deviance involve maximization; and (3) demonstrate how our theory explains these behaviors. In this chapter, our focus is on defective products and the acts of the tobacco industry. While this chapter does not analyze all forms of corporate violence, we are confident that our theory likely explains most forms of it.

FORMS OF ELITE DEVIANCE

Defective Products

Defined

Defective products include any good or service that is unreasonably dangerous to those who purchase the good or service. More than twenty-three million defective products are likely being used by consumers in the United States alone.[2] These products are considered defective because they have the potential to seriously injure or kill the users. The word "defective" is generally understood to mean imperfect or faulty.

According to the US Consumer Product Safety Commission (CPSC)—which is charged with "protecting the public from unreasonable risks of serious injury or death from more than 15,000 types of consumer products"—the total cost associated with defective products in the United States is $700 billion every year! This cost includes "deaths, injuries and property damage from consumer product incidents."[3]

In 2007, the CPSC employed less than five hundred employees who were responsible for monitoring the safety of more than fifteen thousand kinds of consumer products. Like most regulatory agencies, the CPSC has fewer employees and less money than in the past, because of deregulation of businesses by Congress in the 1980s.

According to its website, the CPSC "is committed to protecting consumers and families from products that pose a fire, electrical, chemical, or mechanical hazard or can injure children." It works to "ensure the safety of consumer products—such as toys, cribs, power tools, cigarette lighters, and household chemicals."[4]

Although the true extent of injuries and deaths that can be attributed to defective products cannot be reliably known, experts agree that far more people are injured and killed from defective products each year than from all street crimes combined. Murder kills approximately 16,000 people per year and violent street crimes cause physical injuries to less than 1 million people. Further, the most common violent street crime is assault, which typically does not lead to any serious injury requiring hospital treatment.[5]

It is known that even though more than one thousand products are recalled each year, more than 20,000 people in the United States are killed annually by defective products. This number is understood to represent the minimum killed by defective products, for it excludes the 438,000 who die each year from tobacco-related illnesses, the approximately 300,000 who die from eating high fat diets (including large amounts of fast food products) and not exercising enough, the more than 100,000 who die from adverse reactions to legal and approved drugs, and the 60,000 who die each year due to toxic chemicals.[6]

An estimated 30 million Americans are injured each year by defective products, as well. For example, nearly 200,000 children require emergency room care for toy-related injuries, and more than 2 million people suffer from serious reactions to approved drugs. The Centers for Disease Control and Prevention (CDC) estimates that food-borne diseases, caused by pathogens such as *Listeria*, *Salmonella*, and *Toxoplasma*, lead to more than 75 million illnesses, 325,000 hospitalizations, and 5,000 deaths every year in the United States.[7]

The dangers of defective products cannot be overstated. Often, even after a recall, products end up back in the hands of additional consumers because they are resold to unknowing customers rather than being destroyed.

Examples

Defects occur in all kinds of products, ranging from food products, drugs, medical devices, automobiles, household products, toys, and even cosmetics. David Friedrichs acknowledges that some products are just inherently dangerous, but then asserts, "much evidence suggests that corporations, in their almost single-minded pursuit of profit, have been negligent—sometimes criminally negligent—in their disregard for consumer safety."[8]

Consumer protection agencies such as *Consumer Reports* provide information on recently recalled products.[9] The frequency with which products are recalled is simply stunning, and includes hundreds of cars, sports utility vehicles (SUVs), trucks and vans; children's toys; dozens of appliances; lawn products; car seats; electronic devices; home improvement and home furnishing products; as well as several types of foods and beverages; drugs and health products; some household products such as automatic garage door openers; and ironically, some safety products such as gun trigger locks and carbon monoxide and smoke detectors. Some defective products even involve those aimed at protecting police, such as some bullet-proof vests, as well as some devices meant to protect society from criminals, such as electronic monitoring bracelets.

It has been alleged that other products, including some intended for the most vulnerable consumers (such as child safety seats) are defectively designed, shoddily manufactured, and inadequately tested by regulatory agencies. Similar claims have been made against some baby cribs. Such products cause thousands of deaths and hundreds of thousands of injuries annually in the United States.

Some specific kinds of foods have been addressed in the realm of defective product legislation and regulation. For example, beef was considered very unsafe before the 1970s despite several federal laws requiring safety and inspection standards. Even today, meat inspectors are understaffed and meat plants are rarely inspected. In the late 1990s, the federal government declared that *E. coli* bacteria (*Escherichia coli* O157:H7) was an epidemic because it was so widespread in the nation's meat. Part of the reason bacterial infections of meat are so common is because of how the meat is processed. Meat packing plants run at a very fast and unsafe speed, increasing the risk of disease spreading from fecal matter and stomach contents of the animals to the carcasses.[10] The speed of the assembly line also contributes to thousands of employee injuries every year, making the meat-packing industry among the most dangerous in America.[11]

Automobiles are frequently found to be defective in one of two ways: first, there are design defects that are discovered by corporations and not fixed; second, corporations routinely resist safety devices until forced to adopt them by public demand. [12] Examples of the latter include resisting putting in safety windshields and air bags. Yet, the most well-known case of a defective product involved a car that was known by its manufacturer to be defective but was not recalled for the purpose of saving the company money.

The most well-known case of a defective product is the Ford Pinto. This automobile was manufactured in the 1970s despite the findings of precrash tests that showed rear-end collisions were rupturing fuel lines. Ford knew about these test results, but learned that it would cost $11 per car to fix the automobiles and calculated that it could save $87.5 million by not fixing the cars.[13] This was based on the assumption that hundreds of people would be killed and injured and thousands of cars burned at minimal costs to the company. Unfortunately for the company and its customers, Ford underestimated the prevalence of the crashes and the size of the civil judgments against it.

In this case, the company simply reasoned that fixing a known product defect would cost more than letting people die in fiery crashes. David Simon explains: "Although the company calculated that it would cost only $11 to make each car safe, it decided that this was too costly. Ford reasoned that 180 burn deaths, 180 serious burn injuries, and 2,100 burned vehicles would cost $49.5 million (each death was calculated at $200,000). The $200,000 figure was created by the National Highway Traffic Safety Administration (NHTSA) "under pressure from the auto industry."[14] But doing a recall of all Pintos and making each $11 repair would amount to $137 million. Thus, to save money, Ford chose not to fix the cars and instead to market them and sell them to would-be victims. Table 5.1 shows the actual dollar figures used by Ford to calculate that it would be cheaper to let people burn and die in their cars than to fix the Pinto and save lives.

Table 5.1. Ford Cost–Benefit Analysis with the Pinto

BENEFITS

Savings: 180 burn deaths, 180 serious burn injuries, 2,100 burned vehicles.
Unit Cost: $200,000 per death, $67,000 per injury, $700 per vehicle.
Total Benefit: 180 × ($200,000) + 180 × ($67,000) + $2,100 × ($700) = $49.5 million.

COSTS

Sales: 11 million cars, 1.5 million light trucks.
Unit Cost: $11 per car, $11 per truck.
Total Cost: 11,000,000 × ($11) + 1,500,000 × ($11) = $137 million.

Source: Ford Motor Company internal memorandum. Fatalities associated with crash-induced fuel leakage and fires. *Mother Jones,* September/October 1977. Retrieved from www.motherjones.com/news/feature/1977/09/death.html.

In this case, Ford engineer Dennis Gioia explained his failures to recognize the defect in the Pinto and the company to recall the car.[15] His main argument is that the corporate scripts that guided thinking and activity about models such as the Pinto precluded consideration of morality and ethics because they simply did not include them.

Ford had a more recent problem with defective products when the Firestone tires on its Ford Explorer models were rupturing on the road and caused drivers to flip and crash their SUVs, often being seriously injured or killed. When evidence began to mount that there was a problem, Ford was slow to recall its product in the United States even though it had already done so in more than a dozen countries a year earlier. Further, Ford did not alert the National Highway Transportation Safety Administration (NHTSA), as required by federal law, when employees in other countries found defects in Firestone tires on their cars (nineteen months prior to the U.S. recall).[16]

Although the CEOs of Ford and Firestone blamed each other for the problems, evidence suggests it was the unique combination of Firestone tires on Ford Explorers that was the problem. The tires were subject to likely rupture (and so many customers were told to drive with underinflated tires), but the Ford Explorer had a high center of gravity and thus was subject to likely rollovers after tire rupture. Ford denied responsibility but subsequently redesigned the Ford Explorer for "a smoother ride." Ford widened the wheel base and lowered the car (both having the effect of lowering the center of gravity), which reduced the risk of rollover accidents.

Amazingly, this is not the first time there has been a serious problem with Firestone tires. In the 1970s a problem of tread separation was noted in Firestone tires. After the problem was discovered by Firestone and NHTSA, the company continued to make, advertise, and sell the product. Under intense pressure to do something about the tire, Firestone decided to sell off the tires at clearance prices! Even though the tires caused thousands of accidents, hundreds of injuries, and thirty-four known deaths, the company was fined a mere $50,000![17]

Documents internal to these companies show that they were aware of the problems and kept them secret, and that it took years for the defects to finally come to light. This is typical in defective products cases. Other examples of defective automobile products include General Motors (GM)–approved conversion vans that become deadly after the original steel roofs are replaced; defective seatbelts and seatbelt buckles in some GM and Ford cars; faulty backdoor latches in Chrysler minivans that opened when struck from the rear or side and caused passengers to be thrown from the vehicle; and GM sidebag and sidesaddle gas tanks that were located on the side of trucks, outside of the protective frame, and easily ruptured when struck from the side. The sidebag and sidesaddle gas tanks have caused more fatalities than any other vehicle product.[18]

In 1992, NHTSA asked GM to voluntarily recall pickup trucks with such gas tanks. GM refused and the Department of Transportation secretary discovered in 1994 that GM knew about the defect since the 1970s. GM entered into a deal with the Department of Justice to avoid a recall and has paid hundreds of millions of dollars in settlements to victims instead. Thousands of these vehicles are still on the road.[19]

Another well-known case of a defective product is the Dalkon Shield, an intrauterine birth-control device inserted in millions of women in the 1970s. This device was not only ineffective but was also dangerous because it allowed bacteria to enter the uterus, causing spontaneous and septic abortions, birth defects, and even deaths of women. The company that manufactured the product knew about it yet did not repair the product, replace it, or stop advertising it to women.[20]

Silicone breast implants are another well-known device marketed to women. The FDA stated that the safety of these products was unknown even though they were already being used. Documents show that scientists worried about the safety of these products and that the manufacturer had evidence of the ruptures that allowed silicone to leak into the body causing serious illness long before such ruptures were widespread in the 1990s. Similar claims were verified against the makers of Rely tampons in the 1980s, which were linked to toxic shock syndrome in women who used them. Toxic shock produces fever, rashes, skin peeling, low blood pressure, respiratory distress, shock, and even death.[21]

With the exception of the Ford company, which was acquitted at trial in the Pinto case, the makers of each of the above products were ordered by courts to pay billions of dollars to compensate victims. Not one corporate executive went to jail or prison.

Injuries and deaths caused by defective products do not include those attributable to poor health care, pollution, and food additives.[22] Nor do they include deaths caused by the chemical additives in food or adulterated food products.[23] Nor do they include deaths and illnesses attributed to consumption of too much fast food, high-fat foods, sugary foods, high-salt foods, and so forth, each of which is heavily marketed to consumers, especially children.[24] Studies show that nearly all (90 to 100 percent) of advertisements for food on television during shows intended for kids (e.g., Saturday morning cartoons) promote sugar-coated cereals, candies, and other unhealthy snacks, and literally none advertise fruits and vegetables and other healthy foods.[25]

David Simon indicates that advertising aimed at kids is "effective because the advertisers have done their research. Social science techniques have been used by motivation researchers in laboratory situations to determine how children of various ages react to different visual and auditory stimuli. Children are watched through two-way mirrors, their behavior is photographed, and their autonomic responses (for example, eye pupil dilation) are recorded to see what sustains their interest, their subconscious involvement, and the degree of pleasure that they experience. Thus, advertisers have found that if one can associate fun, power, or a fascinating animated character with a product, children will want that product."[26] The McDonald's "Happy Meal" is a great example.

Some would likely claim that many of the foods Americans consume can be considered defective, in that they are extremely dangerous due to high-fat and saturated-fat content, high levels of cholesterol, high calories, and deficiencies in important vitamins and minerals. Eric Schlosser's (2002) *Fast Food Nation* documents the harmful nature of most types of fast food, with a focus on McDonald's. He documents the numerous perks and incentives the McDonald's corporation has received from Congress in order to succeed within, and ultimately come to dominate, the fast food industry; the numerous additives (including chemicals) used to flavor popular foods; how likely it is that consumers are consuming fecal matter in their hamburgers; as well as how dangerous the work in the nation's meat packing industry is.[27]

Greg Critser's (2004) *Fat Land: How Americans Became the Fattest People in the World* demonstrates how more than 60 percent of Americans have become overweight and more than 20 percent have become obese, as well as the various illnesses and costs this imposes on society. More important, he discovers that much of the blame lies with corporations, particularly producers and marketers of unhealthy products and product sweeteners such as high fructose corn syrup.[28]

Even school lunches are unhealthy. Marion Nestle, in *Food Politics: How the Food Industry Influences Nutrition and Health* (2007), puts much of the blame on the food industry. Its lobbying and public relations activities, advertising (including to children in schools), placement of soft-drink vending machines in schools, and promotion of heavy portions of high-fat foods produces bad outcomes for children. She also points out that food companies promote overeating, even knowing the risk this poses.[29] Michelle Simon's (2006) *Appetite for Profit* demonstrates that the motivation for the nation's major food companies is greed—fast profit without regard for the health consequences of their actions.[30]

Pharmaceutical corporations have promoted their drugs even after determining that the drugs were dangerous. At times, the "corporations put the pursuit of profits ahead of scrupulous concern for the health and safety of the users of their products."[31] One can see dozens of pharmaceutical ads every day on television and in magazines that promote the use of drugs for a wide variety of ailments. The companies encourage consumers to talk to their doctors about the drugs (rather than having the doctors suggest drugs and other forms of treatment based on the nature of conditions actually suffered by their patients). Sometimes the drugs' side effects sound worse (and may be worse) than the conditions they are meant to treat. At other times, the drugs are promoted for use by children even though they have not been tested on children (e.g., drugs to treat "mental illnesses" in kids).

Testing results are not reported to the public, nor are they required to even be reported to the Food and Drug Administration (FDA). And the pharmaceutical industry often conducts its own tests and/or pays doctors and medical researchers to conduct the tests for them, raising the potential for conflicts of interest.[32]

The most recent example of defective products involved the most vulnerable of all consumers—children. Millions of toys have been recalled in the past year by major corporations such as Mattel, Fisher-Price, and Toys "R" Us, among others, due to excessive lead levels, especially in toys produced in China.

David Barboza asks: "Why is lead paint—or lead, for that matter—turning up in so many recalls involving Chinese-made goods? The simplest answer, experts and toy companies in China say, is price. Paint with higher levels of lead often sells for a third of the cost of paint with low levels. So Chinese factory owners, trying to eke out profits in an intensely competitive and poorly regulated market, sometimes cut corners and use the cheaper leaded paint."[33] That is, the company values profit over human safety and life.

As a result of the vast recalls, studies have been undertaken to examine toys for hazardous materials, including but not limited to lead. One study found high lead levels common in hundreds of toys, and the vast majority of toys have not been recalled. Further, there are dangerous levels of other kinds of chemicals in children's toys besides lead. Healthytoys.org has a list of toys by type with results from product tests.[34]

The organization tested more than twelve hundred children's products as well as more than three thousand product components. They found that "[l]ead in products is widespread." Specifically, lead was detected in 35 percent of tested products, including 38 percent of the jewelry samples. Whereas the maximum recommended exposure to lead is 40 parts per million (ppm), the tests showed that 17 percent of products tested were at levels above 600 ppm.[35] Some of the most highly advertised and popular toys were found to be unsafe.

Additionally, the tests revealed other dangerous chemicals in children's toys. Dangerous chemicals found in high levels included cadmium, arsenic, and mercury. Many of the toys were even made from dangerous materials such as polyvinyl chloride (PVC) plastic. The organization says: "PVC is the worst plastic from an environmental health perspective because it creates major hazards in its manufacture, product life and disposal and contains additives that are dangerous to human health. PVC plastic without additives is a very brittle plastic. In order to make it flexible and to give it other properties, additional chemicals must be added. Phthalates are very commonly added to PVC to make it soft and flexible; however, they can leach out of the plastic. Phthalates have been implicated in some health problems in laboratory tests. Lead, cadmium and other heavy metals are also commonly added to PVC products."[36] In Table 5.2, Healthytoys.org highlights why information on dangerous toys is vital to parents and consumers.

How Defective Products Involve Maximization

Corporations that make and sell products are engaged in legal activity in pursuit of the American Dream (conformity). When manufacturers knowingly market and sell defective products and/or fail to initiate actions that lead to a product recall, the corporations' deviant activities (innovation) are committed simultaneously with the legal activities protected by the law. This is maximization.

According to the CPSC: "Manufacturers have it in their power to design, build, and market products in ways that will reduce if not eliminate most unreasonable and unnecessary hazards. Manufacturers are best able to take the longest strides to safety in the least time; . . . competitive forces may require management to subordinate safety factors to cost considerations, styling, and other marketing imperatives."[37]

Typically, corporations that make defective products do not adequately test their products to make sure they are safe. When they do and discover

Table 5.2. Why Information about Toys Is Important to Parents and Consumers

- There is no premarket approval process for the use of chemicals in toys or other consumer products to ensure they are safe.
- Despite all we know about the dangers of lead and other toxic chemicals, manufacturers are allowed to use them in toys and other children's products when safer alternatives exist.
- Weak consumer product safety laws force the Consumer Product Safety Commission (CPSC) to rely largely on voluntary consumer product standards developed by industry groups. CPSC has little authority and virtually no existing regulations to enforce chemical limits in toys. The agency has a tiny staff that is inadequate to provide effective oversight.
- Current laws and policies regulating toxic chemicals in toys and other products are reactive in nature. The system lacks requirements for toy and consumer product manufacturers to test products for most chemical hazards. This problem is compounded by the lack of toxicity information on most chemicals in commerce.
- Tests have verified that some toys contain chemicals of concern including heavy metals such as lead and cadmium. In nearly all cases, the presence of these toxic chemicals in consumer products is perfectly legal in the United States.
- The only U.S. law restricting lead in toys applies only to paint. And, other than that lead paint standard, currently the only standard for a small group of toxic chemicals in children's toys is a voluntary industry standard that cannot be enforced. Children's jewelry is ineffectively regulated, and jewelry with high levels of dangerous chemicals is commonly found on store shelves.
- The U.S. government doesn't require full testing of chemicals before they are added to most consumer products, including children's toys. And once they are on the market, the government almost never restricts their use, even in the face of new scientific evidence suggesting a health threat.

Source: Healthytoys.org. Retrieved from www.healthytoys.org/about.why.php.

defects, at times they may simply fail to make corrections to the product, alert the CPSC, or recall the product. Even worse, sometimes companies simply choose to market products they know are defective or dangerous, such as juice contaminated with bacteria, cars like the Ford Pinto, medical products like the Dalkon Shield birth-control device, and dozens of drugs intended to treat various medical conditions.[38] Scholars have even presented evidence that companies have knowingly produced false test results to muddy the issue of product safety. This is another example of maximization.

Like with the Ford Pinto, in many alleged cases of defective products we consistently see attempts by corporations to withhold information from the public and to minimize potential harms posed by their products. It is also common for corporations to arrange secret settlements with victims that prevent other consumers from protecting themselves against defective products and to delay payments when settlements are reached. These are other examples of maximization.

The Tobacco Industry

Defined

Tobacco has a long and celebrated place in America's history. Many cities in southern states like Virginia and North Carolina were literally built around the tobacco industry. Thousands upon thousands of people there made a living growing, treating, selling, and marketing tobacco to smokers. Cigarette smoking was widely popular in Hollywood movies as well as among consumers for decades.

The tobacco industry is made up of several large companies that are in the business of packaging, marketing, and selling various forms of tobacco products to consumers, most notably cigarettes. Some of the leading companies in the United States include Philip Morris and R.J. Reynolds Tobacco Company.

In 2006, only 21 percent of Americans smoked cigarettes, down from 42 percent in 1964. As research started demonstrating the harmful nature of smoking to those who use cigarettes (as well as to those exposed to "secondhand smoke"), smoking has become less and less popular over time. Today, smoking is highest among the poor, the less educated, and is slightly more likely among African Americans than Caucasians. Further, smoking is most common among young people, like those in high school.[39]

Tobacco use is the leading cause of preventable death in the United States, making cigarettes the most commonly recognized defective product in the United States. Cigarettes are considered defective products by many because they kill and cause illness when used properly. According to the Centers for Disease Control and Prevention, smoking "harms nearly every organ of the body; causing many diseases and reducing the health of smokers in general."[40] As the leading cause of preventable death in the United States, cigarette smoking kills roughly 438,000 people every year in America (about one in five deaths).[41] Smoking will kill approximately 25 million Americans who are currently alive, including about 5 million children.[42] Smoking is more deadly than the human immunodeficiency virus (HIV), motor vehicle accidents, suicides, murders, and all deaths caused by alcohol and all illegal drugs combined![43] Further, smokers will die, on average, fourteen years earlier than nonsmokers.[44]

The largest portion of smoking deaths are the result of lung cancer (124,000 deaths), heart disease (108,000 deaths), and emphysema, bronchitis, and chronic airways obstruction (90,000 deaths).[45] The CDC claims that "the risk of dying from lung cancer is more than 22 times higher among men who smoke cigarettes and about 12 times higher among women who smoke cigarettes compared with never smokers."[46] Further, smoking "results in a twofold to threefold increased risk of dying from coronary heart disease"[47] as well as a "tenfold increased risk of dying from chronic obstructive lung disease."[48]

The main reason smoking is so dangerous is that there are roughly four thousand chemicals and sixty known carcinogens found in tobacco smoke. Table 5.3 lists some of the known ingredients in tobacco smoke. Tobacco

Table 5.3. Some of the Chemicals in Tobacco Smoke

Acetic acid (a caustic solvent found in vinegar)
Acetone (a poisonous solvent found in nail polish remover)
Acrolein (an aquatic herbicide)
Ammonia (a cleaning agent and poisonous gas)
Aniline (an industrial solvent)
Butane (cigarette lighter fluid)
Cadmium (as in rechargeable batteries)
Carbon dioxide (as in global warming)
Carbon monoxide (as in auto exhaust)
Catechol (a tanning and dyeing agent)
DDT/Deildrin (insecticides)
Ethanol (alcohol)
Formaldehyde (the fluid used to embalm bodies)
Formic acid (a caustic solvent)
Glycolic acid (a metal cleaning agent)
Hexamine (barbecue lighter)
Hydrazine (a rocket fuel chemical)
Hydrogen cyanide (as in rat poison and the poison used in the gas chamber)
Hydroquinone (a photographic developing agent)
Lactic acid (a caustic solvent)
Methane (swamp gas)
Methyl chloride (a poisonous refrigerant)
Methylamine (a tanning agent)
Nicotine (an addictive drug and insecticide)
Methylpyridine (an insecticide solvent)
Napthalene (from mothballs)
Nitrobenzene (a gasoline additive)
Nitrous oxide phenols (a disinfectant)
Phenol (a toilet disinfectant)
Polonium-210 (a radioactive element)
Pyridine (a poisonous solvent)
Quinoline (a specimen preservative)
Stearic acid (candle wax)
Succinic acid (an agent in lacquer manufacturing)
Toluene (an industrial solvent in explosives)
Vinyl chloride (used to make PVC)
Zinc (an anticorrosion coating for metals)

Source: About.com (2007). What's in a cigarette? Retrieved November 9, 2007, from quit smoking.about.com/cs/nicotineinhaler/a/cigingredients.htm; Government of British Colombia (2003). What is in cigarettes? Retrieved November 9, 2007, from www.health.gov .bc.ca/ttdr/.

companies also add some pretty unusual ingredients to make them taste better and to preserve freshness.[49]

Tobacco smoking is a leading cause of cancer. Specifically, the CDC reports that

- The risk of dying from lung cancer is more than twenty-two times higher among men who smoke cigarettes and about twelve times higher among women who smoke cigarettes compared to nonsmokers.
- Cigarette smoking increases the risk for many types of cancer, including cancers of the lip, oral cavity, pharynx, esophagus, pancreas, larynx (voice box), lung, uterine cervix, urinary bladder, and kidney.
- Rates of cancers related to cigarette smoking vary widely among members of racial/ethnic groups but are highest among African American men.[50]

Tobacco smoking is also a leading cause of heart disease and stroke. The CDC reports that

- Smoking causes coronary heart disease, the leading cause of death in the United States. Cigarette smokers are two to four times more likely to develop coronary heart disease than nonsmokers.
- Cigarette smoking approximately doubles a person's risk for stroke.
- Cigarette smoking causes reduced circulation by narrowing the blood vessels (arteries). Smokers are more than ten times as likely as nonsmokers to develop peripheral vascular disease.
- Smoking causes abdominal aortic aneurysm.[51]

In addition to the previous conditions, tobacco smoking also threatens respiratory health. The CDC asserts that

- Cigarette smoking is associated with a tenfold increase in the risk of dying from chronic obstructive lung disease. About 90 percent of all deaths from chronic obstructive lung diseases are attributable to cigarette smoking.
- Cigarette smoking has many adverse reproductive and early childhood effects, including an increased risk for infertility, preterm delivery, stillbirth, low birth weight, and sudden infant death syndrome (SIDS).
- Postmenopausal women who smoke have lower bone density than women who never smoked. Women who smoke have an increased risk for hip fracture than never smokers.[52]

Smoking during pregnancy has also been associated with

- Pregnancy complications
- Premature birth

- Low-birth-weight infants
- Stillbirth
- Sudden infant death syndrome (SIDS)[53]

Studies also show that children born to mothers who smoked while pregnant have increased risks of antisocial behavior, juvenile delinquency, and even adult criminality.[54] Of course, it is now well known that cigarette smoking kills more than just smokers. Secondhand smoke is also very dangerous. Secondhand smoke—which is commonly referred to as "environmental tobacco smoke"—"is a complex mixture of gases and particles that includes smoke from the burning cigarette . . . and exhaled mainstream smoke."[55] The CDC claims that secondhand smoke contains "at least 250 chemicals known to be toxic, including more than 50 that can cause cancer."[56]

The detrimental health effects of exposure to secondhand smoke include heart disease and lung cancer, immediate harm to the cardiovascular system, respiratory distress in children, as well as "sudden infant death syndrome (SIDS), acute respiratory infections, ear problems, and more frequent and severe asthma attacks in children." The CDC says: "There is no risk-free level of secondhand smoke exposure. Even brief exposure can be dangerous."[57] There simply is "no risk-free level of exposure to secondhand smoke."[58] Secondhand smoke is a known human carcinogen, according to the Environmental Protection Agency, National Institutes of Health National Toxicology Program, and the International Agency for Research on Cancer. Further, the National Institute for Occupational Safety and Health says that secondhand smoke is an occupational carcinogen.[59]

Not surprisingly, the CDC asserts that secondhand smoke causes lung cancer.[60] Specifically, it causes lung cancer in people who have never smoked. Exposure to secondhand smoke at home or work can increase the risk of lung cancer by 20 to 30 percent. This alone leads to approximately three thousand lung cancer deaths every year.[61]

Secondhand smoke also leads to increase risks of heart disease which produces death.[62] The CDC estimates that secondhand smoke kills between 22,700 and 69,600 people from heart disease every year.[63] Exposure to secondhand smoke immediately produces adverse effects on the cardiovascular system, including the blood and blood vessels.[64] It also interferes with "the normal functioning of the heart, blood, and vascular systems in ways that increase the risk of a heart attack." Amazingly, at least for "some of these negative effects, the immediate impact of even short exposures to secondhand smoke appears to be almost as large as that observed in active smokers."[65]

Finally, secondhand smoke can lead to sudden infant death syndrome (SIDS), which is the "sudden, unexplained, unexpected death of an infant in the first year of life." SIDS happens to be the leading cause of death in healthy infants after one month of age.[66]

Examples of Wrongdoing by Tobacco Companies

Studies of tobacco companies' activities and their internal documents show that major tobacco corporations purposely misled the public and Congress for more than forty years about the dangers of smoking cigarettes; that they intentionally marketed to children and adolescents through cartoon characters such as "Joe Camel" as well as through product advertisements in magazines, movies, and popular hangouts; that they increased the addictiveness of their products through adding nicotine and chemicals that heightened the effects of nicotine; that they attacked and attempted to discredit antismoking advocates and whistle-blowers; that they lied under oath to Congress when asked about the addictiveness of their products; that they financially coerced companies making smoking-cessation products; and even intentionally funded and produced faulty science through their own Tobacco Institute to cloud the significant issues.[67] Studies of tobacco products also showed they have their greatest impacts on kids.[68] While all this was going on, hundreds of thousands of Americans died every year from using the defective products manufactured and sold by tobacco companies.

In the late 1990s, major tobacco companies entered into a financial agreement with the states to pay hundreds of billions of dollars in compensatory damages to states over decades. The money was to be used for various purposes, including preventing youth smoking; in reality, the money has been used by states for various costs completely unrelated to smoking as they struggled with large deficits. Tobacco companies subsequently raised the prices of their products and passed the costs on to their customers. Civil juries in some states have found tobacco companies liable for reckless disregard for human life, outrageous conduct, negligence, misrepresentation of the facts, fraud, and even selling a defective product. Perhaps an editorial in the *Journal of the American Medical Association* (JAMA) said it best when it concluded that "the evidence is unequivocal—the U.S. public has been duped by the tobacco industry."[69]

How the Tobacco Industry Involves Maximization

Clearly, tobacco use is far more deadly than all street crime combined. Cigarettes—a delivery device for the addictive drug of nicotine—are the most deadly consumer product on earth. Tobacco kills more people annually (approximately 438,000) than murder (approximately 16,000) and causes more financial loss (more than $75 billion in direct health care costs) than all street crime combined (about $20 billion).[70] Whereas murder by definition is intentional, manufacturing and promoting the use of tobacco for the specific purpose of killing people is not intentional. Yet, lawsuits against the tobacco industry have shown that the tobacco industry's products have produced hundreds of thousands of deaths in the United States each year.

For a person (or company) to be held responsible for its actions, it must be committed with *culpability*. Recall from chapter 1 that culpability includes acts that are committed *intentionally*, *negligently*, *recklessly*, or *knowingly*. Are tobacco companies responsible (i.e., culpable) for any harms suffered by users of their products? That is, have they acted intentionally, negligently, recklessly, or knowingly in way that has led to harm? Yes.

While some of the behaviors of major tobacco companies are explicitly illegal, others are merely deviant. Some are intentional, others are negligent and reckless. Corporations can be also held liable for their harmful acts. For example, section 2.07 of the Model Penal Code suggests that corporate agents can be held responsible for harms inflicted in the course of their work, including harms resulting from a failure to act, and for actions authorized, performed, or recklessly tolerated by the board of directors.[71] Table 5.4 shows that a corporation may be convicted of the commission of an offense under certain circumstances.

Probably more than any other industry, actions by executives at large tobacco companies best represent the concept of maximization. The corporate culture of big tobacco—referring to the beliefs, values, and norms

---

Table 5.4.   When Corporations Can Be Convicted of Crimes

a. the offense is a violation or the offense is defined by a statute other than the Code in which a legislative purpose to impose liability on corporations plainly appears and the conduct is performed by an agent of the corporation acting in behalf of the corporation within the scope of his office or employment, except that if the law defining the offense designates the agents for whose conduct the corporation is accountable or the circumstances under which it is accountable, such provisions shall apply; or

b. the offense consists of an omission to discharge a specific duty of affirmative performance imposed on corporations by law; or

c. the commission of the offense was authorized, requested, commanded, performed or recklessly tolerated by the board of directors or by a high managerial agent acting in behalf of the corporation within the scope of his office or employment.

Further, a person can be held legally accountable for any conduct he performs or causes to be performed in the name of the corporation.

Source: Model Penal Code.

that dictate its corporate practices and the behaviors of its employees—is criminogenic. Although the companies make a legal product in pursuit of the American Dream (conformity), they simultaneously and regularly engage in reckless, negligent, and knowing behaviors that lead to the deaths of hundreds of thousands of Americans every year. Some of this advertising is illegal, some deviant (innovation). Tobacco companies accept and promote norms in favor of conformity and innovation, simultaneously. And they regularly use both in producing, advertising, and selling their products. If they marketed their products to adults only, using only honest claims, this would not be consistent with maximization. Yet, since they simultaneously engage in criminal and deviant means to achieve wealth (innovation), their behavior exemplifies maximization.

HOW DEFECTIVE PRODUCTS AND THE ACTIONS OF BIG TOBACCO ARE EXPLAINED BY CONTEXTUAL ANOMIE/STRAIN THEORY

Defective products and the activities of tobacco companies are explained by contextual anomie/strain theory (CAST). Recall that contextual anomie/strain theory attributes criminality to a prioritization of the goals associated with the American Dream over the legitimate means to achieve those goals (Robert Merton's anomie theory); frustrations produced by goal blockage whereby individuals are unable to achieve the goals associated with the American Dream, regardless of how much they have (Merton's strain theory); a prioritization of the economy over other noneconomic institutions in America (Steven Messner and Richard Rosenfeld's institutional anomie theory); and greater presence of opportunities for deviance in some situations than in others (Richard Cloward and Lloyd Ohlin's differential opportunity theory). Further, there are additional conditions within the context of the corporation whereby individuals, groups, and subcultures are subjected to added pressures to innovate.

Defective products and the activities of tobacco companies occur because of greed, and greed arises out of the dual pressures exerted on individuals within the corporate subculture as well as by other societal institutions that promote attainment of wealth over any and all other valuable goals. In American society, the welfare of the economy is given priority over all other institutions. The cultural goals of the American Dream are learned in schools and promoted by parents and the polity, acting as surrogates for corporate and capitalistic interests. We all, to some degree or another, subjugate our own interests in order to pursue the goals of the American Dream, even if and when it interferes with the health and happiness of our families. This creates enormous pressure on individuals to pursue the American Dream, no matter the means available for achieving it.

Clearly, these pressures are not sufficient to explain greedy behaviors such as manufacturing and selling defective products and tobacco (both forms of maximization), because most people who experience societal pressures do not regularly engage in making dangerous and defective products. However, these pressures do promote greedy behaviors (some of them criminal, some not) by individuals, as well as within corporations.

Recall from chapter 4 that our argument asserts that maximization occurs because of the additional pressures operating on individuals within the corporation. In corporations, the primary means of satisfying greed by elites is maximization—using illegitimate means (i.e., criminality, deviance) in conjunction with legitimate means (i.e., work). That is, elites simultaneously engage in innovation and conformity to achieve even greater wealth. We have shown in this chapter that maximization is accepted, expected, and even celebrated within American corporations. It is the *de facto* means of succeeding and excelling. It is normal.

The corporate subculture that has emerged as corporations have gained more and more strength and prominence in American society encourages and at times mandates elite deviance through maximization. Further, it provides justifications for forms of elite deviance such as manufacturing defective and deadly products through maximization. Individuals neutralize their bond to societal rules as well as personal morals as they pursue the corporate mandated goal of outlandish levels of wealth.

Reiterating from chapter 4, it is important to keep in mind that corporate crime involves entities that promote their own interests above those of the individuals who make up the corporation. In this context, individual morals and values are superseded by corporate interests and ultimately become irrelevant; individuals are contractually obliged to pursue the best interests of the corporation (even when they conflict with social good); loyalty to the corporation significantly impacts individual behavior; true social responsibility is illegal; in some cases such as the Ford Pinto, individual employees act according to routinized scripts rather than direct orders from management; and over time, legitimate and illegitimate means of pursuing wealth and the American Dream become blurred and simply unimportant.

NOTES

1. Cullen, Francis, Gray Cavender, William Maakestad, and Michael Benson (2006). *Corporate Crime Under Attack: The Fight to Criminalize Business Violence.* Cincinnati, OH: Anderson, 25.

2. Consumer Product Safety Commission (2007). CPSC overview. Retrieved November 8, 2007, from www.cpsc.gov/about/about.html.

3. Consumer Product Safety Commission, CPSC overview.

4. Consumer Product Safety Commission, CPSC Overview.

5. Robinson, Matthew (2005). *Justice Blind? Ideals and Realities of American Criminal Justice* (2nd ed.). Upper Saddle River, NJ: Prentice Hall.

6. Robinson, Matthew B. (2006). Defective products. *Encyclopedia of Corporate and White-Collar Crime*. Golson Books and Sage Publications.

7. Robinson, Defective products.

8. Friedrichs, David (2006). *Trusted Criminals: White Collar Crime in Contemporary Society* (3rd ed.). Belmont, CA: Wadsworth, 75.

9. Consumer Reports (2007). Recalls. Retrieved November 11, 2007, from www.consumerreports.org/cro/consumer-protection/recalls/childrens-products/index.htm.

10. Schlosser, Eric (2002). *Fast Food Nation: The Dark Side of the All-American Meal*. New York: Harper.

11. Human Rights Watch (2004). *Blood, Sweat, and Fear: Workers' Rights in U.S. Meat and Poultry Plants*. Retrieved January 31, 2008, from www.hrw.org/reports/2005/usa0105/usa0105.pdf; Schlosser, Eric (2001). The chain never stops. *Mother Jones* (July/August). Retrieved January 31, 2008, from www.motherjones.com/news/feature/2001/07/meatpacking.html.

12. Robinson, Defective products.

13. Robinson, Defective products.

14. Mother Jones (1977). What's your life worth? Retrieved January 31, 2008, from www.motherjones.com/news/feature/1977/09/worth.html.

15. Gioia, Dennis A. (1992). Pinto fires and personal ethics: A script analysis of missed opportunities. *Journal of Business Ethics* 15(5/6): 379–89.

16. Rosoff, Stephen, Henry Pontell, and Robert Tillman (2002). *Profit Without Honor: White-Collar Crime and the Looting of America* (2nd ed.). Upper Saddle River, NJ: Prentice Hall, 99.

17. Simon, David (2006). *Elite Deviance* (8th ed.). Boston, MA: Allyn & Bacon, 135.

18. Robinson, Defective products.

19. Robinson, Defective products.

20. Robinson, Defective products.

21. Robinson, Defective products.

22. Reiman, Jeffrey (2006). *The Rich Get Richer and the Poor Get Prison* (8th ed.). Boston, MA: Allyn & Bacon.

23. Simon, *Elite Deviance*, 149.

24. Friedrichs, David (2006). *Trusted Criminals: White Collar Crime in Contemporary Society* (3rd ed.). Belmont, CA: Wadsworth, 75; Simon, *Elite Deviance*, 141–42.

25. Simon, *Elite Deviance*, 142.

26. Simon, *Elite Deviance*, 142.

27. Schlosser, *Fast Food Nation*.

28. Critser, Greg (2004). *Fat Land: How Americans Became the Fattest People in the World*. New York: Houghton Mifflin.

29. Nestle, Marion (2007). *Food Politics: How the Food Industry Influences Nutrition and Health* (2nd ed.). Berkeley, CA: University of California Press.

30. Simon, Michelle (2006). *Appetite for Profit: How the Food Industry Undermines Our Health and How to Fight Back.* New York: Nation Books.

31. Friedrichs, *Trusted Criminals*, 77.

32. Angell, Marcia (2005). *The Truth about the Drug Companies: How They Deceive Us and What to Do about It.* New York: Random House; Brody, Howard (2007). *Hooked: Ethics, the Medical Profession, and the Pharmaceutical Industry.* New York: Rowman & Littlefield; Crista, Greg (2007). *Generation Rx: How Prescription Drugs Are Altering American Lives, Minds, and Bodies.* New York: Mariner Books; Law, Jacky (2006). *Big Pharma: Exposing the Global Healthcare Agenda.* New York: Carroll & Graf; Moynihan, Ray, and Alan Cassels (2006). *Selling Sickness: How the World's Biggest Pharmaceutical Companies Are Turning Us All into Patients.* New York: Nation Books; Weber, Leonard (2006). *Profits Before People? Ethical Standards and the Marketing of Prescription Drugs.* Bloomington, IN: Indiana University Press.

33. Barboza, David (2007). Why lead in toy paint? It's cheaper. *New York Times,* September 11. Retrieved September 11, 2007, from www.nytimes.com/2007/09/11/business/worldbusiness/11lead.html.

34. See Healthytoys.org at www.healthytoys.org/product.searchtype.php.

35. Healthytoys.org (2008). Findings. Retrieved January 31, 2008, from www.healthytoys.org/about.findings.php.

36. Healthytoys.org, Findings.

37. Simon, *Elite Deviance*, 132.

38. Simon, *Elite Deviance*, 136.

39. Centers for Disease Control and Prevention (2007). Percentage of adults who were current, former, or never smokers, overall and by sex, race, Hispanic origin, age, education, and poverty status. Retrieved November 9, 2007, from www.cdc.gov/tobacco/data_statistics/tables/adult/table_2.htm.

40. Centers for Disease Control and Prevention (2007). Fact sheet. Health effects of cigarette smoking. Retrieved November 8, 2007, from www.cdc.gov/tobacco/data_statistics/Factsheets/health_effects.htm.

41. Centers for Disease Control and Prevention (2002). Annual smoking-attributable mortality, years of potential life lost, and productivity losses—United States, 1997–2001. *Morbidity and Mortality Weekly Report* [serial online] 51(14): 300–3 [cited 2006 Dec 5]. Retrieved from www.cdc.gov/mmwr/preview/mmwrhtml/mm5114a2.htm; Centers for Disease Control and Prevention (2003). Health United States, 2003, with chartbook on trends in the health of Americans. Hyattsville, MD: CDC, National Center for Health Statistics [cited 2006 Dec 5]. Retrieved from www.cdc.gov/nchs/data/hus/tables/2003/03hus031.pdf.

42. U.S. Department of Health and Human Services (1989). Reducing the health consequences of smoking—25 years of progress: A report of the Surgeon General. Atlanta, GA: U.S. Department of Health and Human Services, CDC, DHHS Pub. No. (CDC) 89–8411 [cited 2006 Dec 5]. Retrieved from profiles.nlm.nih.gov/NN/B/B/X/S/.

43. Centers for Disease Control and Prevention, Annual smoking-attributable mortality; McGinnis J., W. H. Foege (1993). Actual causes of death in the United States. *Journal of the American Medical Association* 270: 2207–12.

44. Novotny T. E., and G. A. Giovino (1998). Tobacco use. In R. C. Brownson, P. L. Remington, and J. R. Davis (eds.). *Chronic Disease Epidemiology and Control.* Washington, DC: American Public Health Association, 117–48 [cited 2006 Dec 5].

45. Centers for Disease Control and Prevention, Annual smoking-attributable mortality.

46. U.S. Department of Health and Human Services (1998). Tobacco use among U.S. racial/ethnic minority groups—African Americans, American Indians and Alaska Natives, Asian Americans and Pacific Islanders, and Hispanics: A report of the Surgeon General. Atlanta, GA: U.S. Department of Health and Human Services, CDC [cited 2006 Dec 5]. Retrieved from www.cdc.gov/tobacco/data_statistics/sgr/sgr_1998/index.htm.

47. U.S. Department of Health and Human Services, Tobacco use among U.S. racial/ethnic minority groups.

48. U.S. Department of Health and Human Services, Reducing the health consequences of smoking.

49. For examples, see British American Tobacco (2007). Tobacco ingredients. Retrieved November 9, 2007, from www.bat-ingredients.com/servlet/PageMerge?m ainurl=%2Fgroupms%2Fsites%2FBAT%5F6X3ENK%2Ensf%2FvwPagesWebLive %2FDO6X3GEX%3Fopendocument%26amp%3BSKN%3D1%26amp%3BTMP%3 D1; Philip Morris (2007) Product facts. Cigarette ingredients. Retrieved November 9, 2007, from www.philipmorrisusa.com/en/product_facts/ingredients/ingredients_ in_cigarettes/tobacco_ingredients.asp.

50. Centers for Disease Control and Prevention (2007). Cancer. Retrieved November 8, 2007, from www.cdc.gov/tobacco/health_effects/cancer.htm.

51. Centers for Disease Control and Prevention (2007). Heart disease and stroke. Retrieved November 8, 2007, from www.cdc.gov/tobacco/health_effects/heart.htm.

52. Centers for Disease Control and Prevention (2007). Respiratory health. Retrieved November 8, 2007, from www.cdc.gov/tobacco/health_effects/respiratory.htm.

53. Centers for Disease Control and Prevention (2007). Smoking during pregnancy. Retrieved November 8, 2007, from www.cdc.gov/tobacco/health_effects/pregnancy.htm.

54. See the many studies reported in Robinson, *Why Crime?*

55. National Toxicology Program (2000). 11th report on carcinogens, 2005. Research Triangle Park, NC: U.S. Department of Health and Human Sciences, National Institute of Environmental Health Sciences [cited 2006 Sep 27]. Retrieved from ntp. niehs.nih.gov/ntp/roc/eleventh/profiles/s176toba.pdf.

56. National Toxicology Program, 11th report on carcinogens, 2005.

57. U.S. Department of Health and Human Services (2006). The health consequences of involuntary exposure to tobacco smoke: A report of the Surgeon General. Atlanta, GA: U.S. Department of Health and Human Services, Centers for Disease Control and Prevention, Coordinating Center for Health Promotion, National Center for Chronic Disease Prevention and Health Promotion, Office on Smoking

and Health [cited 2006 Sep 27]. Retrieved from www.surgeongeneral.gov/library/ secondhandsmoke/report.

58. American Cancer Society. Cancer facts and figures 2006. Atlanta, GA: American Cancer Society [cited 2006 Oct 23].

59. U.S. Environmental Protection Agency (1992). Respiratory health effects of passive smoking: Lung cancer and other disorders. Washington, DC: Environmental Protection Agency, Office of Research and Development, Office of Health and Environmental Assessment [cited 2006 Oct 23]. Publication No. EPA/600/6-90/006F. Retrieved from oaspub.epa.gov/eims/eimscomm.getfile?p_download_id=36793; U.S. Department of Health and Human Services (2000). 9th report on carcinogens. Research Triangle Park, NC: U.S. Department of Health and Human Sciences, Public Health Service, National Toxicology Program [cited 2006 Oct 23]; International Agency for Research on Cancer (2004). *IARC Monographs on the Evaluation of Carcinogenic Risks to Humans: Tobacco Smoke and Involuntary Smoking*, vol. 83. Lyon, France: International Agency for Research on Cancer [cited 2006 Oct 23].

60. Centers for Disease Control and Prevention (2006). Fact sheet. Secondhand smoke causes lung cancer. Retrieved November 8, 2007, from www.cdc.gov/tobacco/ data_statistics/Factsheets/LungCancer.htm.

61. U.S. Department of Health and Human Services, The health consequences of involuntary exposure to tobacco smoke; also see: American Cancer Society, Cancer facts and figures 2006.

62. Centers for Disease Control and Prevention (2007). Fact sheet. Secondhand smoke causes heart disease. Retrieved November 8, 2007, from www.cdc.gov/tobacco/ data_statistics/Factsheets/HeartDisease.htm.

63. California Environmental Protection Agency (2005). Proposed identification of environmental tobacco smoke as a toxic air contaminant. Sacramento, CA: California Environmental Protection Agency, Office of Environmental Health Hazard Assessment [cited 2006 Oct 23].

64. U.S. Department of Health and Human Services, The health consequences of involuntary exposure to tobacco smoke.

65. Centers for Disease Control and Prevention, Secondhand smoke causes heart disease.

66. Centers for Disease Control and Prevention (2006). Fact sheet. Secondhand smoke causes sudden infant death syndrome. Retrieved November 8, 2007, from www.cdc.gov/tobacco/data_statistics/Factsheets/Sids.htm.

67. Rosoff, Pontell, and Tillman, *Profit Without Honor*, 91.

68. Rosoff, Pontell, and Tillman, *Profit Without Honor*, 149.

69. Reiman, *The Rich Get Richer*, 88.

70. Robinson, *Justice Blind?*

71. Robinson, *Justice Blind?*

6

Conclusions and Policy Implications

The corporation is an externalizing machine, in the same way that a shark is a killing machine. There isn't any question of malevolence or of will. The enterprise has within it, and the shark has within it, those characteristics that enable it to do that for which it was designed.

—Robert Monks, in the film *The Corporation* (2003).[1]

The Corporation is a film documentary based on Joel Bakan's book, *The Corporation: The Pathological Pursuit of Power*.[2] Among the claims of the work are the following:

- Corporations are required by law to elevate their own interests above those of others, making them prone to prey upon and exploit others without regard for legal rules or moral limits.
- Corporate social responsibility, though sometimes yielding positive results, most often serves to mask the corporation's true character, not to change it.
- The corporation's unbridled self-interest victimizes individuals, the environment, and even shareholders, and can cause corporations to self-destruct, as recent Wall Street scandals reveal.
- Despite its flawed character, governments have freed the corporation from legal constraints through deregulation, and granted it ever greater power over society through privatization.[3]

In convincing terms, the author of the book and the makers of the film argue that corporations are doing what they were designed to do—earn large profits without regard for human welfare or safety, and relentlessly pursue massive profits without feeling any guilt or remorse over harms they cause. In essence, corporations act as psychopaths. A *psychopath* can be identified using Robert Hare's Psychopathy Checklist-Revised (PCL-R), which ranks people on twenty traits such as glib and superficial charm, grandiose (exaggeratedly high) estimation of self, need for stimulation, pathological lying, cunning and manipulativeness, lack of remorse or guilt, shallow affect (superficial emotional responsiveness), callousness and lack of empathy, parasitic lifestyle, poor behavioral controls, impulsivity, irresponsibility, failure to accept responsibility for own actions, and criminal versatility.[4]

In his book *Without Conscience: The Disturbing World of the Psychopaths among Us* Robert Hare argues that in our society, some of the traits of a psychopath (such as egocentricity, lack of concern for others, superficiality, and manipulativeness) are not only tolerated but also valued.[5] The corporation is one place where psychopaths are commonly found, and the characteristics of psychopathy also tend to characterize corporations themselves.[6]

In this chapter, we summarize our theory of elite deviance—contextual anomie/strain theory—and briefly discuss how it likely can be used to explain this reality of corporations. We also briefly address additional forms of elite deviance and suggest that our theory is well suited to explain these as well. We also discuss the issue of social justice and explain how it is related to some of our thinking about corporate crime and deviance. Finally, we lay out some possible policy implications of our theory with regard to crime prevention.

SUMMARY OF CONTEXTUAL ANOMIE/STRAIN THEORY

Contextual anomie/strain theory (CAST) is aimed at explaining elite deviance (crimes of the powerful), particularly corporate crime, which as we demonstrated is far more dangerous and common than street crime. The theory builds on Robert Merton's anomie theory, Merton's strain theory, Steven Messner and Richard Rosenfeld's institutional anomie theory, as well as Richard Cloward and Lloyd Ohlin's theory of differential opportunity. As such, it attributes criminality to pressures associated with living in America. Specifically, we see corporate crime emerging because of a prioritization of the goals associated with the American Dream over the legitimate means to achieve those goals; frustration produced by goal blockage whereby individuals are unable to achieve the goals associated with the American Dream, regardless of how much they have; prioritization of the economy over other noneconomic institutions in America; and greater presence of opportunities for deviance in some situations than in others (such as in the workplace).

Further, contextual anomie adds an explicit focus on additional pressures that occur in given contexts in American society, such as within corporations.

On the one hand, Americans are encouraged to be greedy—to seek more than they need, to pursue greater and greater wealth even after "making it," "winning the game," and so forth. On the other hand, some people are encouraged further to be greedy as a result of the contexts or situations in which they find themselves. For example, corporations are designed to maximize wealth, and as it turns out, this is their only expectation. Greed in the corporation is the norm.

The primary means of satisfying greed by elites is *maximization*—using illegitimate means (i.e., criminality, deviance) in conjunction with legitimate means (i.e., work). That is, elites simultaneously engage in what Robert Merton called "innovation" and "conformity" to achieve even greater wealth. As we showed in our analysis of corporations and different forms of corporate crime, maximization is accepted, expected, and even celebrated in given contexts in corporations. The psychopathic behaviors that characterize corporate crime are normal.

In our book, we have demonstrated that maximization is learned and promoted in the corporate subculture, which encourages and at times mandates elite deviance through maximization, as well as provides justifications for elite deviance. We also showed that the likelihood of maximization is contingent upon other factors such as individual personality characteristics, social and personal controls, degree of reward and threat of punishment, loyalty, ideology of executives, and opportunity.

Corporate crimes like fraud, false advertising, defective products, as well as deviant acts by tobacco companies, involve entities that promote their own interests beyond that of the individuals who make up the corporation. In this context, individual morals and values are superseded by corporate interests and ultimately become irrelevant. Individuals working for corporations are contractually obliged to pursue the best interests of the corporation (even when they conflict with social good). Loyalty to the corporation significantly impacts individual behavior, meaning employees often "go along" with illegal and deviant behaviors to keep their jobs, get a promotion, and so on. Further, true social responsibility by the corporation is illegal, meaning, we should not expect corporations to do the right thing in the first place. Over time, within corporations, legitimate and illegitimate means of pursuing wealth and the American Dream become blurred and simply unimportant. That is, corporations pursue wealth by the most efficient means possible, whether they are legal or illegal, normal or deviant. The corporation is a pathologically deviant entity.

HOW OUR THEORY CAN EXPLAIN
OTHER FORMS OF ELITE DEVIANCE

While our analysis was limited to only a handful of corporate crimes, including fraud, deceptive advertising, defective products, and the activities of big tobacco, we are confident that our theory accounts for many other forms of elite deviance. In reading extensively about property crimes such as tax evasion, price fixing, price gouging, embezzlement, insider trading, we believe these are other forms of maximization that are motivated in large amount by greed.[7] Other acts of violence by elites also are illustrative of maximization and are motivated by greed, including physical damage caused to society by deadly pollutants.[8] So too are crimes such as public corruption, election fraud, unfair labor practices, human rights violations, many state crimes, and even many war crimes.[9]

We are not attempting to say our theory can explain every form of elite deviance, but rather that we would not be surprised if many other forms of corporate and state criminality involve simultaneous use of legal and illegal means of opportunity that is motivated in large part by greed in pursuit of the American Dream.

One good example is workplace violence. By workplace violence, we are not referring to the gunman who barges in the front door at work and begins shooting up the place, but rather acts of elites that lead to deaths of employees. The most common sources of death for workers are illnesses contracted at work; illnesses include brown lung (byssinosis), which is often caused by particles found in cotton dust within textile factories,[10] silicosis (caused by exposure to silica dust as found in blasting operations and glass factories), black lung (suffered by coal miners), and asbestosis (caused by exposure to asbestos).[11]

Workers also regularly die at businesses that are frequently cited for safety regulation violations.[12] An example is the twenty-six miners who died in an explosion in Letcher County, Kentucky. The company they worked for had been cited 652 times for violations, including 60 for inadequate ventilation (which caused methane to build up in the mine allowing the explosion to occur). A similar case in West Virginia in 2006 led to the deaths of twelve miners, this time due to a lack of oxygen after a collapse. The company these men worked for had been cited more than 200 times for safety violations and even had to suspend operations 16 times for not following safety rules.[13]

According to Jeffrey Reiman, who painstakingly analyzes available data on workplace violence, 50,000 people die each year due to occupational diseases, and another 250,000 contract job-related serious illnesses.[14] Another 5,000 or so die each year at work, and about 2.8 million people are seriously injured enough at work to have to miss work days.[15] This means at least

55,000 people die each year from occupational disease and injury and more than 3 million become seriously ill or are seriously injured at work. Others claim that 100,000 people die every year due to exposure to toxic substances at work.[16]

Clearly, this kind of workplace violence is an example of maximization, for by definition employing people is a legitimate activity utilized to pursue wealth. The deviant and illegal practices that produce much of the death, injury, and illness among employees are illegitimate and occur simultaneously to the legal means, making it maximization. The motivation for "cutting corners" by endangering workers is profit. Often, it is simple priority—managers place the profit of the corporation before the safety and welfare of its own employees. At times, the workers know they are taking risks and still choose to work in dangerous conditions. Yet, when the corporation is reckless or negligent or acts in way knowing that an outcome is likely, it is culpable for the negative outcomes that result.

Although some of the injuries, deaths, and illnesses could be blamed on the workers themselves, "a substantial portion of workers' deaths, injuries, and diseases are caused by the violation of prevailing laws and regulations."[17] Given all the specific cases described in the literature, scholars are confident that as many as half of all injuries and deaths of workers are caused by corporate negligence and recklessness, and in some cases "laws are broken intentionally."[18]

Jeffrey Reiman dismisses the criticism that people who die at work are to blame, writing: "To say that some of these workers died from accidents due to their own carelessness is about as helpful as saying that some of those who died at the hands of murderers deserved it. It overlooks the fact that, when workers are careless, it is not because they love to live dangerously. They have production quotas to meet, quotas that they themselves do not set. If quotas were set with an eye to keeping work at a safe pace rather than keeping the production-to-wages ratio as high as possible, it might be more reasonable to expect workers to take the time to be careful."[19]

In the case of asbestos, juries have found conclusively that companies had intentionally hidden the risks of asbestos exposure from their employees.[20] One company—the Manville Corporation—hid the dangers of its product for decades as part of its costs–benefits analyses, "concealing information about the health hazards even from its own workers."[21]

Similarly, coal mining companies have typically denied responsibility for the illnesses and deaths of their employees, even after ignoring federal requirements for safe levels of dust particles in the air of the mines. To show additional malice, however, they have also submitted fraudulent samples to government regulators when it has been requested.[22]

According to Stephen Rosoff, Henry Pontell, and Robert Tillman, "in tough economic times, management is more apt to tolerate hazardous equipment, neglect safety precautions, ignore dangerous conditions, and disregard the welfare of workers. Safety, it seems, does not necessarily pay. After all, workers' compensation benefits are relatively inexpensive, and fines for fatal accidents are insignificant for big corporations."[23]

On top of such callousness, corporations often employ child labor, illegal immigrant labor, and Chinese labor in order to cut costs. While employing children and illegal immigrants is illegal, shutting down American factories and relocating production to China (as well as other countries) is not illegal. We contend all of this exemplifies maximization, however, since even employment of foreigners to produce products to be sold in America often involves great amounts of deviance, including low wages, long hours, poor housing, massive environmental pollution, and use of lead paint in many of the products. All the while, corporations are getting richer and richer through maximization, with little effort by regulatory agencies to hold them accountable for their wrongdoings.

CORPORATIONS AND SOCIAL JUSTICE

Some will react to the assertions in this book by claiming that Americans actually owe corporations a major debt, since without corporations we would not be able to enjoy the wide variety of goods and services we have today, not to mention our comfortable standards of living. Leaving aside the issue of which (small) portion of the goods and services that we use we actually *need*, the great bulk of the benefits created by corporations are enjoyed by a small group of people.

Interestingly, these gains are largely not based on merit. Even when companies crash and burn, CEOs of major corporations make out like bandits. For example, Kmart CEO Charles Conaway received $23 million in compensation over two years, after which Kmart filed for bankruptcy, 283 stores closed, and twenty-two thousand people lost their jobs. Tyco CEO Dennis Kozlowski received $467 million in compensation over four years, after which Tyco's stock holders lost $92 billion. Enron CEO Kenneth Lay earned more than $100 million the year before Enron's collapse, after which Enron lost $68 billion, five thousand people lost their jobs, and workers lost $800 million.[24]

CEO salaries are outlandishly high relative to the average employee. In 2006, the average CEO of a major company (earning at least $1 billion in annual revenue) was paid an average of $42,400 every day, or $10.98 million per year. This is approximately 262 times what the average worker at these companies made, which was $41,861 in 2005. Stated differently, the average worker made about $400 less for an entire year's salary than the average CEO made every single day of the year! Further, the salaries of these CEOs were more than 364 times that of the average American worker.[25]

From 2000 through 2005, CEO salaries grew 84 percent. During this same time, workers' salaries fell approximately 0.3 percent![26] In other words, the gap between the rich and the poor—called *income inequality*—is growing. And the gap in salary does not fully capture the true disparities between the highest paid and the lowest paid employees because it does not include the numerous perks received by CEOs. In 2006, the CEOs of America's top twenty companies were paid an average of $438,342 in perks annually, not including pension benefits.[27]

In 2006, CEOs at major U.S. corporations earned an average of $1.3 million in pension gains. Amazingly, only about 59 percent of American households led by a forty-five- to a fifty-four-year-old and 36 percent of households headed by individuals sixty-five years and older report having any retirement account; the annual growth and total amount of such accounts is quite small by comparison to CEOs.

The top twenty highest paid CEOs earned an average of $36.4 million in 2006, which is "38 times more than the 20 highest-paid leaders in the non-profit sector and 204 times more than the 20 highest-paid generals in the U.S. military."[28] Yet, this pales in comparison to the top twenty private equity and hedge fund managers, who made an average of $657.5 million per year in 2006—22,255 times the average salary of American workers![29]

Are such inequalities justifiable? Opinion polls show that not only do Americans find CEO salaries unacceptable, most CEOs also do not think they are warranted. A poll conducted by researchers from a leading business website found that 77 percent of employees and 64 percent of CEOs view CEO salaries as excessive.[30]

Importantly, leading social justice theorists agree. *Social justice* deals with the distribution of good (advantages) and bad (disadvantages) in society, and more specifically with how these things should be distributed within society.[31] Some of the advantages relevant for social justice include money, property, jobs, education, medical care, child care, care for the elderly, honors and prizes, personal security, housing, transportation, and opportunities for leisure. Some of the disadvantages include military service, dangerous work, and other hardships.[32]

Whether something is just or unjust thus depends on whether advantages and disadvantages are distributed appropriately in society. Theorist David Miller explains that when "we attack some policy or some state of affairs as socially unjust, we are claiming that a person, or more usually a category of persons, enjoys fewer advantages than that person or group of persons ought to enjoy (or bears more of the burdens than they ought to bear), given how other members of the society in question are fairing."[33]

Social justice is also about assuring the protection of equal access to liberties, rights, and opportunities, as well as taking care of the least advantaged members of society. Thus, whether something is just or unjust depends on whether it promotes or hinders equality of access to civil liberties, human rights, opportunities for healthy and fulfilling lives, as well as whether it allocates a fair share of benefits to the least advantaged members of society.[34]

The latter conception of social justice comes from theorist John Rawls. His *justice as fairness* posits the following major principles of justice related to liberty and opportunity:

1. Each person has the same indefensible claim to a fully adequate scheme of equal basic liberties, which scheme is compatible with the same scheme of liberties for all.
2. Social and economic inequalities are to satisfy two conditions: first, they are to be attached to offices and positions open to all under conditions of fair equality of opportunity; and second, they are to be to the greatest benefit of the least advantaged members of society.[35]

Just because Rawls's conception of social justice values equality, this does not mean that equal outcomes will be achieved in society, or that they even can be. In fact, Rawls's second principle asserts that inequalities in society are acceptable as long as they meet two conditions. First, as per his "equal opportunity principle," inequalities are acceptable if every person in society has a reasonable chance of obtaining the positions that lead to the inequalities. An example would be equal opportunity to achieve any job. Rawls specifies that "fair equality of opportunity" requires "not merely that public offices and social positions open in the formal sense, but that all should have a fair chance to attain them."[36]

Further, Rawls is very explicit beyond this, saying that "certain requirements must be imposed on the basic structure beyond those of the system of natural liberty. A free market system must be set within a framework of political and legal institutions that adjust the long-run trend of economic forces so as to prevent excessive concentrations of property and wealth, especially those likely to lead to political domination."[37] Beyond political domination, extreme concentrations of wealth "are likely to undermine fair equality of opportunity [and] the fair value of the political liberties."[38] Stated differently, pursuit of excessive wealth through greed is inconsistent with social justice.

The second condition related to the "difference principle" states that inequalities in society must be organized so that they are to the greatest benefit of the least advantaged members of society. After explaining that today's economic inequalities are simply not acceptable, Rawls explains the difference principle this way: "To say that inequalities in income and wealth are to be arranged for the greatest benefit of the least advantaged simply means that we are to compare schemes of cooperation by seeing how well off the least advantaged are under each scheme, and then to select the scheme under which the least advantaged are better off than they are under any other scheme."[39] With two competing arrangements of incomes in a society, the fairer of the two—and therefore the more just of the two—is the one that is to the greatest benefit of the least advantaged.

For example, if in one arrangement, the most well-off class (e.g., chief executive officers) received compensation in the amount of $11 million per year (like today) while the least well-off (e.g., minimum wage workers) were paid a salary of $11,700 (like today) and in another the most well-off received compensation in the amount of $1 million dollars per year while the least well-off were paid a *living wage* (i.e., enough money to pay all meaningful living expenses, which varies by state and even by county), the second arrangement would be to the greatest advantage of the least advantaged and thus the most just.

Justice theorist David Miller agrees that inequalities in society are at times just. There are at least two reasons for this. First, economic inequalities that motivate people to strive for more can sometimes be justified. Second, inequalities may result from differential claims on merit. That is, those individuals who are more meritorious because of their performances deserve more than those who are less meritorious because of their education, skills, and performances. Yet, Miller notes that today's economic disparities are not acceptable. Further, he asserts that citizens believe (1) the gap between the rich and the poor today is too large, (2) the bottom wage is not a *living wage*, and (3) the amount of money being paid to those at the top has not been earned.[40]

To call for a living wage is not to embrace a form of communism or socialism, rather it is based on the recognition that everyone who is working—regardless of job—deserves a salary to provide for basic necessities. Salaries can still be based on education level, skill level, degree of responsibility associated with the job, dangers faced, and so forth.[41] This means social justice is not inconsistent with a market economy.[42] Wade Rowland even says that the problem in corporations is not a problem of capitalism, per se, but instead one of "corporate capitalism"—"capitalism hijacked and dominated by the modern business corporation."[43]

Given these leading theories of social justice, we are confident that greed is inconsistent with social justice. Similarly, we can conclude that maximization by corporations is also not socially just. This is important because it offers hope that government will get serious about holding corporations accountable for their bad behaviors.

CRIME PREVENTION

On top of holding corporations accountable for maximization, we would hope that every effort would be taken to prevent corporate criminality in the first place. Every theory has crime prevention implications.[44] Thus, one can utilize the predictions made by contextual anomie/strain theory to suggest strategies to reduce crime in the United States. Typically, crime prevention involves identifying the factors that make criminality more likely to occur and then creating and implementing efforts to reduce those factors.[45] Although our theory has not yet been subjected to empirical testing, we are confident that the theory is valid given its solid foundation in the literatures on the corporate culture as well as anomie and strain theories, which implicate the broader American culture. Therefore, in the following section, we suggest strategies we might use to reduce criminality given the main propositions of contextual anomie/strain theory.

Contextual anomie/strain theory highlights how America culture is criminogenic. Building on the works of Robert Merton, Steven Messner and Richard Rosenfeld, and Richard Cloward and Lloyd Ohlin, we first acknowledge that criminality arises in our culture, which prioritizes the goals associated with the American Dream (e.g., wealth) over the legitimate means to achieve those goals (e.g., honest work), from frustrations produced by goal blockage whereby individuals are unable to achieve the goals associated with the American Dream regardless of how much they have. Criminality also stems from a prioritization of the economy over other noneconomic institutions in America and a greater presence of opportunities for deviance in some situations than in others. Contextual anomie/strain theory adds that there are conditions within the context of the corporation whereby individuals, groups, and subcultures are subjected to additional pressures to innovate.

As we showed in this book, elites utilize measures of innovation in conjunction with traditional measures of conformity, something we term *maximization*. Maximization takes many forms in the corporate world, including those forms we discussed in this book, such as fraud, deceptive advertising, marketing defective products, and engaging in numerous forms of deviant activity to produce, market, and sell legal products that are highly deadly (such as tobacco).

We attributed maximization to greed, which arises out of the dual pressures exerted on individuals living in America and working within the corporate subculture. Given this, logical crime prevention strategies entail reducing greed in American society as well as in the corporate world. In order for this to happen, we must create measures that would reduce the pressures associated with living in American culture as well as working in the corporate world. The main crime prevention implications of contextual anomie/strain theory include

- Reprioritizing the legitimate means one can use to pursue the American Dream over the value of the American Dream itself—this calls for deemphasizing the significance of wealth and reemphasizing the value of work itself. It also calls for guaranteeing Americans who work full-time, regardless of the nature of work, a "living wage."
- Reducing frustrations produced by goal blockage whereby individuals feel unable to ever achieve the American Dream regardless of how much they have—this entails helping people be satisfied with what they have, especially when their basic needs are already met.
- Reprioritizing the welfare of other noneconomic institutions in America such as the family over of the welfare of the economy—this means truly putting our families first, instead of just saying we are while continuing to sacrifice our most important relationships for the sake of our jobs and the economy.
- Reducing opportunities for deviance in criminogenic situations—in the corporate world, this means increasing regulation of business so that there is real possibility of meaningful oversight to recognize potential for deviant behavior (as well as serious sanctions when it does occur).
- Reducing pressures in the corporation to achieve wealth at any cost—our nation's leaders and business regulators should emphasize doing the right thing in every case, so that hurting consumers is never acceptable practice no matter how much profit can be achieved as a result of such behavior.
- Reemphasizing ethics over profit in the corporate world—this could entail numerous efforts such as requiring ethics classes in the nation's business schools, corporate ethics training, and so forth.

We recognize that these efforts are no small task, for they would require changing American culture itself, as well as changing the way America does business. But corporate capitalism has gone way too far as it is, and much of the profit that has been generated in our current economy is literally built on the property and lives of innocent Americans.

We envision an American society whereby what we have always said is important to us is actually given priority. We envision an American society where we, finally, put our money where our mouth is.

NOTES

1. Big Picture Media Corporation (2003). *The Corporation*. Retrieved February 2, 2008, from www.thecorporation.com.

2. Bakan, Joel (2004). *The Corporation: The Pathological Pursuit of Profit and Power*. New York: Free Press.

3. Big Picture Media Corporation (2008). About the book. Retrieved January 2, 2008, from www.thecorporation.com/index.cfm?page_id=47.

4. Hare psychopathy checklist (2008). Retrieved February 2, 2008, from www.minddisorders.com/Flu-Inv/Hare-Psychopathy-Checklist.html.

5. Hare, Robert (1999). *Without Conscience: The Disturbing World of the Psychopaths among Us*. New York: Guilford Press.

6. Babiak, Paul, and Robert Hare (2006). *Snakes in Suits: When Psychopaths Go to Work*. New York: Regan Books.

7. Friedrichs, David (2006). *Trusted Criminals: White Collar Crime in Contemporary Society* (3rd ed.). Belmont, CA: Wadsworth.

8. Frank, Nancy, and Michael Lynch (1992). *Corporate Crime, Corporate Violence*. New York: Harrow and Heston.

9. Simon, David (2006). *Elite Deviance* (8th ed.). Boston, MA: Allyn & Bacon.

10. Rosoff, Stephen, Henry Pontell, and Robert Tillman (2002). *Profit Without Honor: White-Collar Crime and the Looting of America* (2nd ed.). Upper Saddle River, NJ: Prentice Hall, 160–61.

11. Cullen, Francis, Gray Cavender, William Maakestad, and Michael Benson (2006). *Corporate Crime Under Attack: The Fight to Criminalize Business Violence*. Cincinnati, OH: Anderson, 28.

12. Rosoff, Pontell, and Tillman, *Profit Without Honor*, 167.

13. Cullen et al., *Corporate Crime Under Attack*, 27.

14. Reiman, Jeffrey (2006). *The Rich Get Richer and the Poor Get Prison* (8th ed.). Boston, MA: Allyn & Bacon, 79.

15. Reiman, *The Rich Get Richer*, 139.

16. Simon, *Elite Deviance*, 51.

17. Cullen et al., *Corporate Crime Under Attack*, 26.

18. Cullen et al., *Corporate Crime Under Attack*, 28.

19. Reiman, *The Rich Get Richer*, 79.

20. Cullen et al., *Corporate Crime Under Attack*, 29.

21. Friedrichs, *Trusted Criminals*, 81.

22. Simon, *Elite Deviance*, 51.

23. Rosoff, Pontell, and Tillman, *Profit Without Honor*, 168.

24. Huffington, Arianna (2003). *Pigs at the Trough: How Corporate Greed and Political Corruption Are Undermining America*. New York: Crown.

25. Fair Economy (2007). Americans pay a staggering cost for corporate leadership. Retrieved December 20, 2007, from www.faireconomy.org/press_room/2007/exec_excess_2007_the_staggering_cost_of_corporate_leadership

26. CNNMoney (2006). CEO paycheck: $42,000 a day. Retrieved December 20, 2007, from money.cnn.com/2006/06/21/news/companies/ceo_pay_epi/index.htm.

27. CNNMoney (2007). CEO pay: 364 times more than workers. Retrieved December 20, 2007, from money.cnn.com/2007/08/28/news/economy/ceo_pay_workers/index.htm.

28. CNNMoney, CEO pay.

29. CNNMoney, CEO pay.

30. Yahoo News (2007). Even CEOs think CEOs are overpaid? Retrieved December 20, 2007, from news.yahoo.com/s/nm/20071219/od_nm/survey_dc.

31. Miller, D. (2003). *Principles of Social Justice*. Harvard, MA: Harvard University Press, 11.

32. Miller, *Principles of Social Justice*, 10.

33. Miller, *Principles of Social Justice*, 1.

34. Rawls, J. (2003). *Justice as Fairness*. New York: Belknap Press.

35. Rawls, *Justice as Fairness*, 42–43.

36. Rawls, *Justice as Fairness*, 43.

37. Rawls, *Justice as Fairness*, 43.

38. Rawls, *Justice as Fairness*, 53.

39. Rawls, *Justice as Fairness*, 59–60.

40. Miller, *Principles of Social Justice*, 68–71.

41. Miller, *Principles of Social Justice*, 78, 83.

42. Miller, *Principles of Social Justice*, 109.

43. Rowland, Wade (2005). *Greed, Inc.: Why Corporations Rule Our World and How We Let It Happen*. Toronto, Canada: Thomas Allen Publishers, xix.

44. Lilly, J. Robert, Francis Cullen, and Richard Ball (2006). *Criminological Theory: Context and Consequences* (4th ed.). Thousand Oaks, CA: Sage.

45. Robinson, Matthew (2004). *Why Crime? An Integrated Systems Theory of Antisocial Behavior*. Upper Saddle River, NJ: Prentice Hall.

Index

About the Authors

Matthew Robinson is professor in the Department of Government and Justice Studies at Appalachian State University. He earned his Ph.D. in criminology and criminal justice at the Florida State University in 1997. Robinson teaches and does research in the areas of criminological theory, criminal victimization, the drug war, capital punishment, and injustices of the criminal justice system. He has published more than seventy pieces of research, including nine books. He also has served on the board of directors for the Southern Criminal Justice Association (SCJA), as well as president of SCJA. Robinson has been awarded the William C. Strickland Outstanding Young Scholar Award, the Board of Governors Award for Excellence in Teaching, as well as the Donald Sink Outstanding Scholar Award from Appalachian State University.

Daniel S. Murphy is assistant professor in the Department of Government and Justice Studies at Appalachian State University. He earned his Ph.D. in sociology and criminology from Iowa State University in 2003. Murphy teaches and does research in the areas of criminological theory, criminal justice, corrections, prisons, and public policy. He has published a dozen pieces of research, including articles in some of the discipline's top journals. He is also author of two books. Murphy serves on several notable boards, including FedCure.

CPSIA information can be obtained at www.ICGtesting.com
Printed in the USA
BVOW08s1837190916

462628BV00001B/51/P